Praise for The Passion Plan

"Richard Chang hits the nail on the head! I definitely share his belief that passion is what gets you through the tough times in the pursuit of our goals. My passion for hockey enabled me to enjoy a successful fifteen-year career in the National Hockey League, and still drives me to this day to participate in charity games throughout Canada and the United States."

> —Rick Middleton, NY Rangers/Boston Bruins 1973–88

"In *The Passion Plan*, Richard Chang has created a handbook for turning dreams into reality. Take this book seriously and you can create a better life worth living."

> —Bob Nelson
> President, Nelson Motivation, Inc.
> Author, *1001 Ways to Reward Employees,*
> *1001 Ways to Energize Employees,* and
> *1001 Ways Employees Can Take Initiative*

"Richard Chang boldly challenges us not only to seek and find the passions which exist in all of us, but more importantly equips us with a plan to pursue those passions all the way to a rewarding and fulfilling life."

> —Ken Blanchard, co-author of *The One Minute Manager*®

"Over the last decade or more, I have had the opportunity of observing the rise of Dr. Chang from trainer and consultant to an industry leader among trainer and consultants. He has not only mastered the leadership aspects of professional education, but he has also lived the message in his own career that he shares with you in *The Passion Plan*. I heartily recommend that you take him on as a personal mentor and learn from him through this book."

> —Jim Cathcart
> Author, *The Acorn Principle*
> CEO. Cathcart Institute, La Jolla CA
> Past President of The National Speakers Association

"*The Passion Plan* by Richard Chang rings out with the authenticity of the author's own life experience — one of remarkable success based on his own exuberant passion for life. The book provides a practical roadmap for all who want to gain control over their lives through the discovery and application of their own passion.

> —Ned Herrmann
> Chairman/Founder Herrmann International
> Author of *The Whole Brain Business Book and Creative Brain*

The
Passion Plan

The
Passion Plan

A Step-by-Step Guide to Discovering, Developing, and Living Your Passion

Richard Chang

Jossey-Bass Publishers
San Francisco

The Passion Plan™, the Passion Plan Model™, Passioneer™, and the cover image figure are registered trademarks of Richard Y. Chang. Share your Passion Plan stories and examples by visiting: www.thepassionplan.com.

Chapter 1: Excerpt from *The Prophet* by Kahlil Gibran. Copyright 1923 by Kahlil Gibran and renewed 1951 by Administrators CTA of Kahlil Gibran Estate and Mary G. Gibran. Reprinted by permission of Alfred A. Knopf Inc.

Chapter 2: Excerpt from *The Power of Myth,* by Joseph Campbell with Bill Moyers, edited by Betty Sue Flowers. Copyright © 1988, New York: Anchor Books. Reprinted by permission of Doubleday, a division of Random House.

Chapter 7: Excerpt from *Toward A Psychology of Being,* 2nd ed. by Abraham H. Maslow. Copyright © 1968, New York: Van Nostrand Reinhold. Reprinted by permission of John Wiley & Sons, Inc.

Jossey-Bass books and products are available through most bookstores. To contact Jossey-Bass directly, call (888) 378–2537, fax to (800) 605–2665, or visit our website at www.josseybass.com.

Substantial discounts on bulk quantities of Jossey-Bass books are available to corporations, professional associations, and other organizations. For details and discount information, contact the special sales department at Jossey-Bass.

Printed in United States of America.

Interior design by Paula Goldstein.

Library of Congress Cataloging-in-Publication Data
Chang, Richard Y.
    The passion plan: a step-by-step guide to discovering,
developing, and living your passion / Richard Chang. — 1st ed.
        p. cm. — (The Jossey-Bass business & management series)
    Includes bibliographical references.
    ISBN 0-7879-4813-6 (acid-free paper)
    1. Self-actualization (Psychology) 2. Success—Psychological
aspects. I. Title. II. Series.
    BF637.S4 C484 1999
    158—dc21

                                                                99-6392

first edition
HB Printing   10 9 8 7 6 5 4 3 2 1

Dedication

To my parents William and Catherine, who instilled in me the courage and desire to constantly discover and live my passions. Thank you for your unconditional love and support along the journey.

To my sister Sophia, brother-in-law C. T., and niece Kasen. Thank you all for being there through the successes and challenges I have experienced and will continue to experience from my passion pursuits.

And in loving memory to my godmother, Roberta Ma, whose unending passion for learning, spirituality, and helping others still serves as my continual inspiration to keep passion as the compelling force of everything I do.

Contents

The Author xi
Foreword xiii
Preface xvii
Acknowledgments xxi
Introduction xxiii

Chapter One
Why Passion Works: The Way of the Passioneer 1

Chapter Two
From Passion to Profit: A Model for Success 43

Chapter Three
Step One: Start from the Heart 57
Passion Plan Worksheet #1 73

Chapter Four
Step Two: Discover Your Passions 75
Passion Plan Worksheet #2 110

Chapter Five
Step Three: Clarify Your Purpose 113
Passion Plan Worksheet #3 146

Chapter Six

Step Four: Define Your Actions 149

Passion Plan Worksheet #4 180

Chapter Seven

Step Five: Perform with Passion 183

Passion Plan Worksheet #5 210

Chapter Eight

Step Six: Spread Your Excitement 215

Passion Plan Worksheet #6 241

Chapter Nine

Step Seven: Stay the Course 245

Passion Plan Worksheet #7 271

Chapter Ten

Profit with a Capital P: Reaping Your Rewards 275

References 285

The Author

Richard Chang has always been driven by his passion for personal and organizational excellence. In his youth, he mastered three musical instruments and excelled at a variety of competitive sports—including roller skating, tennis, swimming, water polo, volleyball, and bowling. As a freshman at UCLA, he won the National Collegiate Singles Championship in bowling, was named amateur bowler of the year for Southern California, and bowled on the professional tour.

Chang is now CEO of Richard Chang Associates, Inc., a performance improvement consulting, training, and publishing firm headquartered in Irvine, California. He is internationally recognized for his strategic planning, performance measurement, quality improvement, organization development, product realization, change management, customer service, and human resource development expertise. As an internal business practitioner, he held internal management and senior leadership positions in four organizations. He has served as an external consultant to a wide variety of domestic and international organizations—including Toshiba, Citibank, McDonald's, Universal Studios, Fidelity Investments, Nortel Networks, and Nabisco.

Chang is the author or coauthor of more than twenty books on business and personal development and is the award-winning author of over ten training videotapes. He is the 1999 Chair of the Board for the American Society for Training and Development and has been a judge for the prestigious Malcolm Baldrige National Quality Award. He has a Ph.D. in industrial/organizational psychology and has been cited in Outstanding Young Men of America, Who's Who in Leading American Executives, and International Who's Who in Quality.

In addition to his business experience, Chang has also been a therapist in the private practice and community-clinic settings. As a top-rated and engaging speaker, he addresses a wide range of audiences at conferences and corporate events around the world.

foreword

I am asked to review hundreds of manuscripts every year and rarely find one that moves me enough to endorse it. When Richard Chang, a friend and colleague of mine for many years, showed me this book, I knew it was something extraordinary in the making. Richard has impressed people around the world with his own passion and expertise, and it is reflected in *The Passion Plan*. In a matter of decades, he has established a reputation for integrity that has brought him a tremendous amount of success in the business world.

To learn that his passion is the source of his success comes as no surprise. Many people are so busy trying to rush quickly toward success that they have forgotten what is most important in the process. Rather than basing our success on our passions, what Richard calls our "greatest natural resource," we often try to succeed in spite of those passions. We ignore them, hide from them, and even sometimes come to resent them.

I'm excited about Richard's book because it shows you the consequences of pursuing success without first defining what it really is. Why are people so willing to turn their backs on their passions rather than seizing those passions to use them to benefit themselves and others? In *The Passion Plan*, Richard boldly challenges us to seek and find the passions that exist in us; more important, he equips us with a plan to pursue those passions all the way to a rewarding and fulfilling life.

What Richard has managed to do in the pages of this book is extraordinary. He has tackled a topic that too many see as threatening and chaotic, and he has given it form and substance. In Chapter One, he defines passion and illustrates the many ways it can work to both positive and negative ends in our lives. He then shows us why so many of us have abandoned or ignored our passions while simply striving to live practical lives. This insight alone is a revelation worthy of thought.

Chapter Two is the heart of the book: a seven-step model for bringing passion into your life and using it to build success—based upon your own terms of significance. Throughout the chapter, Richard defines the many benefits of Profit with a capital P. Ironically, many people today find success to be hollow once they achieve it. It doesn't turn out to be what they thought they wanted all along. Profit implies lasting benefits from the entire experience. It is a reward that is simply a product of our passions.

The Passion Plan is not a quick fix or a formula for financial success. It is a plan for life and a source of lasting, positive change. I'm big on getting to the heart of the issue, and the first step in *The Passion Plan* is to "start from the heart." This requires you to change your perspective, to see the world through the lens of your passions. Richard shows you how to do this in simple, easy-to-understand, but meaningful ways. He also illustrates how cultivating your passions opens a world of opportunities for you while creating a rewarding life.

In the seven steps that follow in Chapters Three through Nine, *The Passion Plan* explains in clear and concrete terms how passion can change your life. If you feel you have lost your passion, this plan will show you how to find it. If you have not yet discovered your passions, this plan shows you how to discover them. It helps you define your purpose by following your passions and explains how to effectively put them to work for you.

Finally, Richard illustrates the value of spreading your passion to others, while renewing it in yourself despite being overwhelmed by the constant challenges of this life.

Tomorrow's victories, in business and in life, are directly linked to how you utilize your passions. Those who know, understand, and follow their hearts are able to tap their passions in new and exciting ways. With *The Passion Plan*, Richard Chang equips us with the ability to enjoy our journey into the significant success of the future.

I recommend that you study this plan and use it. You may or may not be heading in the wrong direction. Perhaps you're just moving in slow motion. Or maybe you're not even moving at all. Or you might know what direction you want to head in, but you lack the raw energy and enthusiasm that your passions provide to drive in that direction. Whatever your situation is in life, this book will influence your direction positively.

Read it. Learn from it. Profit from it. But most important—for others as well as yourself—live it.

Ken Blanchard
Coauthor, *The One Minute Manager*®
Escondido, California

Preface

At our core, in our heart, resides all the power we need to bring about any change we may dream of or hope for. Unfortunately, few of us ever tap into it. We fear our heart rather than respect it. We feel vulnerable, exposed, and even foolish when we listen to its whisperings. Rather than embracing our passions, we lock them safely away to be called upon at a more practical time or, more likely, to be lost deep within the recesses of memory. After years of denial and rationalization, we become hardened to existing passions and unable to identify new ones.

In this book, I introduce you to the Passion Plan™, a seven-step process that helps you understand the passion within you and use it to build the life you want. First, I show how to identify your Profit—what you really want in life. I'll further clarify this Profit concept in the Introduction and throughout the book.

Then, I explain how you can discover your passion if it eludes you, or find your passion if you have lost it. Because it is powerful, passion poses certain dangers. So I also explain how to use your passion *wisely* and *effectively*. I show how to focus your passion around a purpose and create a plan for working toward your Profit. I demonstrate how you can keep your passion alive in the face of obstacles and how you can share it with others. Most important, I show you how to do this at your own pace and on your own terms.

By following the Passion Plan, you can do the following:

- Increase your self-awareness
- Bring excitement and enthusiasm into your day-to-day living
- Overcome your limitations and weaknesses
- Improve your performance personally and professionally
- Create opportunities for personal success
- Take control of your happiness
- Find your personal Profit

Through the stories, examples, and tools you are about to enjoy, I hope that you will quickly realize that discovering, developing, and living your passion is part art and part science. By sharing my own personal examples, as well as the examples generously shared by people interviewed during the course of writing this book, I have tried to transform a subjective emotion or feeling like passion into an objective and manageable plan of action.

The path you carve using the Passion Plan will be your own. Once you find your passion, only you can determine where you want it to lead and how you follow it. It might take you away from where you are or it may bond you there more deeply. It might impel you to embrace long-lost desires or seize upon completely new ones. Whatever direction you take, I hope it helps you find the fulfillment we all deserve.

As you progress through the book, I encourage you to make notes and complete the worksheets at the end of the chapters—gradually creating your own Passion Plan. I'm anxious to hear about your personal experiences applying the principles described in *The Passion Plan*. Please visit **www.thepassionplan.com** to share your personal stories about how you've been "living the Passion Plan" and to review examples from other readers, or e-mail your stories to **thepassionplan@rca4results.com.**

Read on. I extend you this challenge: let passion in!

Wishing you success,
Richard Chang
August 1999

Acknowledgments

When I decided to write this book, I knew it had to come more from the heart than the head. It needed to be inspirational, motivational, genuine, realistic, and practical.

Thanks, therefore, to my friends and acquaintances who are quoted or described herein. You are all part of my Passion Plan.

Special thanks go to the following:

- Anne Andrus, my talented writer and researcher, for helping me turn a lifetime of experiences and ideas into a meaningful written message. Her energy and passion made it possible to complete this book.
- The entire team of impassioned associates at Richard Chang Associates, Inc., for encouraging and supporting me throughout the book development process. Each of you has played an important role in helping me live my personal passions. My special thanks to Jill Hennigan, Denise Jeffrey, Dena Putnam, Donna Campbell, Pamela Wade, and Melissa Zirretta, who provided extra support reviewing content, documenting information, designing graphics, and supporting a wide variety of marketing and book completion logistics.

- The team of talented professionals at Jossey-Bass, Inc., for providing the editing, marketing, and production support needed to bring this book to publication. Special thanks to Susan Williams, my gifted editor, for being so collaborative, supportive, and encouraging throughout the manuscript development process; to Julianna Gustafson, Paula Goldstein, and Dawn Kilgore, for providing leadership in the design and production of the book; and to the publicity, sales, and marketing teams for putting this book into the hands of impassioned readers around the world.
- Patti Danos, my skillful publicist, for her encouragement, guidance, and enthusiasm throughout the book publicity process.
- My extended family of relatives, close friends, business colleagues, and clients for supporting, challenging, and believing in me along the way and as I continue to live my passions everyday.

Finally, I acknowledge the readers of this book for having the curiosity, interest, and courage to get in touch with their passions and act on them.

Introduction

LETTING PASSION IN

Man is only truly great when he acts from the passions.
    BENJAMIN DISRAELI, 1884

Not long ago I was asked to facilitate a business planning meeting for senior-level managers at a Fortune 500 company. That's not unusual for me   I'm a business consultant—but this particular meeting made a deep impression. When I asked the executives about management issues in their company, I was amazed. One after another they complained about the company and its procedures and culture. Some complaints were valid, even though the company was excellent and respected for its products and services. But I soon realized that the criticisms voiced were not the true cause of discontent.

After listening to their grievances for fifteen minutes or so, I stopped them. I surveyed the furrowed brows and pursed lips and asked, "If you're all so unhappy, what's keeping you here?" The room fell silent. Their jaws dropped and their eyes widened. The formerly vocal audience was stunned. My question apparently caught them off guard. I continued: "I don't see any balls and chains keeping you here. If you're so miserable, why don't you leave?"

A few moments passed before one director mentioned that she was biding time until retirement. Another cited the generous benefits package the company provided. From the corner, in a tone of utter bewilderment, a vice president responded, "I have no idea why I'm here." Not one member of the group cited actual enjoyment of the job or the feeling of doing something important or worthwhile.

The attitude these managers displayed is not so different from that shared by many people today. We spend a lot of time doing things we don't want to do in places we don't want to be for no other reason than that we feel we have to. We have to bring home a paycheck, please our friends and family, and meet the expectations the world has set for us. If nothing else, we find ourselves in less than ideal situations out of habit. We follow the path our lives begin to take and are too afraid, or reluctant, to change our course as time goes by.

Perhaps in some way this has happened to you. Do you feel stuck in a job or field you dislike? Do you feel stifled by your boss or coworkers? Do you have little or no time to do what really matters to you? Do you wish you could improve the quality of relationships with friends and family members but lack the energy or commitment to do so? Do you long for greater freedom or for new experiences that seem out of reach?

Chances are you answered yes to at least one of these questions. Most do, even when they have a good—if not great—income, the respect of their peers, and the love of their family. Whatever your response, you probably want more. You may not be able to put a finger on it, but you still sense that you are not accomplishing all you can, that fulfillment is eluding you. Are you failing to reach your full potential as a professional or parent? Have you abandoned a dream that part of you aches to realize? Do you yearn to have a more lasting impact on the world? Such feelings might not be burning desires but rather subtle longings that consistently remind you that something else awaits you if only you will work for it.

PROFIT WITH A CAPITAL P

What you hope and dream for, secretly or openly, is what I call "Profit with a capital P." Success, with its traditional connotations of a good salary, a nice home, and a couple of cars in the driveway, is no longer sufficient to represent the scope and complexity of our desires. As we enter a new century and a new millennium, we have come to expect more. We want to profit not only financially but in terms of our emotional, spiritual, physical, interpersonal, and professional experiences. We don't just want a big paycheck, we want to feel good about how we earn it. We want to take pride in our work, be excited about it, and know that we are growing through it. We don't just want to have a few children and send them to college, we want to spend significant time with them, give them every opportunity to discover their talents, and teach them that they too are entitled to more. We don't just want to put in our time only to collect a pension at age sixty-five. We want to work for ourselves, retire on our own terms (if at all), and find new ways to heighten our experiences aside from professional life. In short, we want to create and define our own success. We want to build our own Profit.

Over twenty-five years of counseling individuals and consulting with organizations, I have seen these changes take place. I have also seen people who have redefined success but have been unable to achieve it. They have not found a way to reach their Profit. Instead of being liberated by their dreams and the knowledge that they can make them reality, they are paralyzed by reluctance and uncertainty and overwhelmed by the abundance of choices they face.

The challenge we face today is to overcome our hesitance and take the steps, as the late 1990's Nike ads urged, to "just do it," to bring about our Profit rather than waiting for it to magically appear. But how? If you are like the managers I faced that day, you are stuck by complacency, caution, unawareness, even fear. Something is holding you back, preventing you from living the life you truly want to live.

PASSION IS THE ANSWER

Based on my experience and that of others I have studied, advised, and consulted, I have learned that those able to overcome the deterrents to fulfillment derive their energy and initiative from a single source: passion. That's right, passion. Not the romantic variety, although many argue it certainly cannot hurt, but the kind that fills you with energy and excitement, that gets you up in the morning and keeps you awake at night. When you experience it, you lose track of time and become absorbed in the task at hand. This passion creates personal intensity, uplifts you, and inspires you. It heightens your performance and enables you to achieve things you may never have dreamed possible. Most important, it holds the key to your happiness, to realizing your Profit.

As Benjamin Disraeli said over a century ago, people achieve greatness (and, I contend, happiness) only when they act from their heart and their passion. Those who learn to recognize the promptings of their heart and then find the courage to follow them are the ones who win races, rule nations, and create masterpieces. They also, regardless of their circumstances, live with a sense of contentment and a knowledge that they are who they want to be.

If you are frustrated or disillusioned with your current situation, you might be surprised to learn that others relish their lives and so enjoy their personal and professional existence that they would not change a thing. They fill their waking hours with activities that invigorate and excite them. They perform with a confidence and conviction that distinguishes their efforts as superior. They integrate passion into their lives so successfully that they rarely think to complain. They are at once gratified and satisfied. The magic such people possess is that they do not have to stop and question their happiness or why it has come to pass. They are actively engaged in building their lives by pursuing their passion; they know no other way. I call these people *passioneers*™.

Can you imagine loving your life down to almost the last detail? It seems impossible, doesn't it? Can you imagine jumping out of bed every morning, eager to go about your day-to-day activities because they strike a chord in you, because you love them? Can you picture yourself not wanting to stop at the end of the day? About now you probably doubt me, but you must believe me. I know too many of these people to question their authenticity.

In case you think me overly idealistic, I should explain. Passioneers are not perfect, they are quite human. They are subject to frustration in the face of bureaucracy, sorrow in the face of tragedy, fear in the face of danger. They do not, however, live with regret. They follow their heart and are not afraid to take chances in doing so. They are rich and poor, famous and anonymous, young and old.

Every day I talk to people who ask me the same questions. What should I be doing differently? How do I make a change? How do I find fulfillment when I don't know where to begin? I know I could achieve more, that I could do better, but how? What's the secret? The answer to all these is simple, and it is the secret of the passioneer. *Look to your heart: follow your passion.* That may seem oversimplified, but I stand by it. Your heart holds the answers to all the questions you might ask yourself and reveals them to you through passion.

PASSION IS A CHOICE

The first step in becoming a passioneer is to realize that passion is a choice. You can decide right here, right now, to let passion into your life—just as might a president, an Olympian, or a Nobel Prize winner. *Passion is not a privilege of the fortunate few; it is a right and a power that we all possess.* You might envy those who are fired up about their lives. You may view their success as the product of luck or circumstance, but rarely does either factor play a part. Those who reap the rewards of following their passion do so because they make a conscious choice to integrate it into their lives. Things do not magically happen for them any more than they do for you or me. As passioneers well know, once you infuse your life with passion you create new opportunities and the possibility for changes that others might view as lucky. We control our options and therefore also our outcomes. I am trapped in my job only as long as I choose to stay in it. I am prevented from finding happiness only if I do not seek it. Only when I deem something impossible does it actually become so.

Deciding to follow your heart entails risk. Only you can decide how you will let your passion guide you. Simply acknowledging passion and its validity is a daunting step for many. Wholeheartedly embracing it seems out of the question for most. At any level the choice to follow your heart is frightening. It means setting aside the stifling, yet reassuring, restraints of reason and exposing yourself to the uncertainty of the unknown. But I promise that once you decide to let passion in, the quality of your experience will be so heightened, so enriched, that you will not regret it. Not only will you stand an increased chance of achieving your own vision of Profit, you will enjoy the time spent reaching it.

EXECUTIVE REDUX

In case you think you can't learn or be convinced, let me follow up on my tale of the grumbling executives. When they returned a week later, they were an entirely different group. I had asked them to list the things in their lives that they were excited about, that really meant something to them. Then I asked them to brainstorm a list of areas and functions within the company where they might have the opportunity to pursue some of these passions. Given their former misery I wasn't sure what they would say, but I was pleasantly surprised.

Each was able to identify something he or she would like to pursue in the company. One man realized that one of his passions was competition. He loved the thrill and adrenaline rush he got when focused on winning or achieving a quantifiable result. His position in the finance department offered him little opportunity to do that; he was enduring his position rather than enjoying it. Making his list, he realized he was also uncompetitive in his personal life. He had not created an outlet for his passion. I was not surprised that he felt apathetic not only toward his job but toward life in general.

We discussed his options and came up with a list of possible solutions. He needed to find a place for competition in his life. At work he felt it possible to move from finance to sales and marketing or product development, either of which would be more competitive. As a salesman he could compete for contracts and customers; as a product developer he could focus on creating winning products.

As the day progressed, we developed plans for all the executives to let passion into their work. Some saw opportunities for change in their existing jobs, whereas others felt a new position would be the most effective route. One realized that a more drastic change was necessary—that he was in the wrong company.

You might think the company would resent my intervention, but not so. Within a few months all the managers had improved their performance and become more fulfilled in their jobs. The finance manager left accounting and moved into sales and marketing. Soon his passion expressed itself, and people noticed. He became a star performer; before he was thought average. The changes he made at work were reinforced by changes he made in his personal life. He joined a softball team, and as his family cheered him on he began to play out the passion he had so long repressed.

The changes this man made were relatively minor—taking a new job in the same company, joining a neighborhood team—but they were enough. They created a way for his passion to reenter his life. You can choose to let passion into your life, to become a passioneer.

The
Passion Plan

CHAPTER 1

Why Passion Works

The Way of the Passioneer

We may affirm absolutely that nothing great in the world has been accomplished without passion.
HEGEL, *PHILOSOPHY OF HISTORY*, 1832

W hen I was eight, I knew I had to create and run a business. It had to be my own. I don't know how to explain it, but I knew what I had to do. It was in me, part of me. The other kids on the block dreamed of being a movie star or a baseball player, but I dreamed of becoming a great entrepreneur. I knew I couldn't build a financially successful business empire without experience, so I started a lemonade stand. First I persuaded my mother to give me the recipe and some supplies. Always supportive, she gladly turned over a pitcher, lemons, sugar, ice, and glasses. I hosed down my little red wagon, painted a sign (which I attached to the side), and set off to canvass the streets and find my fortune. My mobile store was so successful I soon enlisted the help of friends. Under my direction they created four more makeshift stands and positioned them strategically on each corner entering neighborhood. With the help of our "Beat the Heat" marketing blitz, we made more money in a few weeks than we could spend on comic books, candy, and Frisbees in a year.

I was not the only kid to start a lemonade stand; doing so was a virtual rite of passage in our free-market economy. My reason, however, was probably different from most. Though my enterprise was successful, I was not simply after money; even then my entrepreneurial passion was so strong I could not ignore it. The desire to create a business burned within me and fueled my imagination. I could not think of any better or more exciting way to fill my time than by building something that people would find useful. Too naïve to doubt myself and unacquainted with inhibition, I simply set my eyes on my goal and went for it.

The story of my passion could have ended as I closed the lemonade stand when school started. I could have graduated from college, worked for a large corporation in an important position, and been prosperous. At any point, I could have chosen to put my passion on the back burner in lieu of a safer route. But I was fortunate enough to stay in touch with my passion, cultivating and growing it over the years. My neighborhood entrepreneurship grew to include a theater group, which performed in front of a blue-flowered backdrop in my friend Sammy's garage and subsisted on entrance fees paid by family and friends. Front-row seats were a dollar; those in rows two through four were fifty cents. Later, I expanded the lemonade stand's product line to include Pixie Sticks, Life Savers, and occasionally the candy bars the school forced us to peddle as a fund-raising activity.

In high school, I found I could pursue my passion in unconventional ways. Academic and extracurricular demands precluded me from selling sugar water on street corners, but not from turning class fund-raisers and the yearbook into moneymakers. As junior class president, I organized fund-raising activities to fill our class bank account so we could fund the prom at the end of the year. In addition, we aggressively solicited advertisements from local businesses. We were so successful that the yearbook turned a profit. Using the proceeds, we were able to pay for many additions: full-color photos, a full-color centerfold, and other new features.

I describe this only to illustrate how passion has always been vital to me. I have always carried out the entrepreneurial passion in some way—throughout college, graduate school, and my professional life. It has always driven me to start new businesses. When working for organizations, I managed departments and work groups that operated in a start-up or entrepreneurial mode. Today my consulting, training, and publishing company advises organizations around the world. I have come a long way from lemons and Life Savers.

I feel fortunate that life's challenges have not robbed me my passion. I sometimes wonder what I would be doing if I had not listened to my heart, if I had chosen a more practical or less demanding path. Perhaps I would have succeeded, but I doubt that I would have the degree of joy and exhilaration in my life as I do now.

FOLLOW YOUR HEART

Asked how I built a business at a relatively young age, I used to provide traditional answers: I worked hard, set goals, never gave up. Then one day it hit me. Those were true, but I received the praise and recognition of my clients and colleagues only because I was following my heart. I continually improved my performance and increased the range of my abilities. I was—and still am—excited by the opportunities each day offers to pursue my passion further. I learn new things about myself and my potential with every experience and constantly find new ways to express my passion. This book is one.

I am not alone. Many others have discovered their passion and followed their heart. Recently, I saw a TV segment on a motocross champ who recognized his passion for racing early and pursued it with great success, winning a national championship when he was young. Along the way he married the longtime girlfriend who had cheered him on unfailingly over the years. Together they traveled the country, living in trailers and hotel rooms so he could compete—not a situation most newlyweds would crave. They were committed to his dream, and despite the obvious stresses enjoyed their time together. But just when everything seemed perfect, a terrible accident put him in the hospital. Doctors said he would never race again. The couple had a new son, so the former champion and his wife felt an obligation to be sensible and heed the doctors' advice. But something told them that he could come back—that he needed to come back. After months of intense therapy and rehabilitation, he proved the doctors wrong. He returned to the circuit with a vengeance, won races, and was well on his way back to another national championship. It seemed nothing could stop him.

His wife, now expecting their second child, and his son watched only months later when—at the same course where he had been injured the year before—he crashed again, this time breaking his arms. Surely now he would have to quit. How, as a husband and father, could he ignore the dangers racing posed? He and his wife seriously considered the possibilities. Finally, after weeks of deliberation, they knew what they had to do. As his wife told a reporter, he had to follow his heart. He couldn't give up on his dreams. You may think that foolish, but the emotions she expressed said it all. She knew he would be unhappy not competing, and with her support the benefits of continuing to race greatly outweighed the costs. Abandoning racing and betraying his heart actually became the more dangerous alternative.

This example is perhaps unusual; the passion involves actual hazard to one's health. And I'm not advising you to race motorcycles, wrestle crocodiles, or dive from cliffs. Passion is not about pursuing challenges or opportunities that are beyond you. It is a gift, something precious to be handled wisely and carefully. It is to be valued, not abused. Only when you weigh the motivations of your heart with the considerations of your head, including the limitations of reality, can you reach your Profit—the goal you really want to achieve in life—without risking your current and future happiness.

THE PASSION CONUNDRUM

Most of us, tragically, never recognize the relationship between head and heart. We are taught to defer to the head in all matters of judgment. But the key for passioneers like the young motocross champion is to start with the heart. Only when people are in touch with their passions do they use their heads to give shape and substance to their dreams. By linking the two in a process of self-evaluation and action, passioneers use their greatest strengths to achieve their greatest goals.

In his landmark work *The Prophet,* Kahlil Gibran (1995 [1923]) wrote, "Your soul is oftentimes a battlefield, upon which your reason and your judgment wage war against your passion and your appetite." Passioneers defy this conflict and set their heads and hearts in harmony. The two can work in tandem. So why do many fall into the category Gibran describes? Why do we let emotion and reason battle for control of our lives rather than harnessing them both to achieve our best?

I think the main reason is that from childhood most of us are taught to fear passion, to view it as dangerous. We are led to believe that there is something dark about it, that it has a sinister element that compels people to commit crimes in its name. That it is irrational and unpredictable. That it brings heartache and regret. We begin to believe that the pursuit of passion is also the pursuit of pain and uncertainty. Why put everything on the line when the payoff might be resounding failure or humiliation? Why bring such risk on ourselves when we can take a much safer and foreseeable path?

These concerns are reinforced by the experiences of many celebrities of our day. How many rock stars have followed their passion for music or fame down a road of self-destruction? How many actors have sought acclaim and fortune only to be rewarded with crisis and despair? All around us are people led astray by passion. No wonder we recoil into safe, comfortable roles—scared of the reckless abandon that is passion.

History, factual or fictional, confirms our fears. What good did passion do Romeo and Juliet? I mean not so much their physical passion as the passion that compelled them to abandon privilege, money, family, and friends to create a life they wanted, even needed, together. Were they rewarded with happiness? No. They died, a tragedy most of us were required to study at great length in school. Is it any wonder in the face of such examples that we learn to be wary of our passions, that we find ways to disguise or repress them?

But I wonder if Shakespeare would have considered it a greater tragedy for Romeo and Juliet to live. Imagine if he scripted them to forsake their love and spend the rest of their days alone and apart. Certainly they would be miserable, but their tragedy would be ordinary. Think about it: they would be ordinary. Tragic, yes, but in an ordinary way. They would become more like the rest of us, fearful of where their passion might lead them. Instead they die in pursuit of something greater; they weigh the risks and view life in defiance of passion as not worth living.

Fortunately, for most of us, following our heart today does not entail great danger or complete rejection of our present lives. We are reluctant nonetheless. We know that passion lurks inside us; we feel tinges of it now and then. If you doubt this, consider the last time you saw a movie or read a book that really moved you. Remember how you felt—elated, uplifted, saddened. You probably left with a spring in your step or pondering the joys and sorrows of life. You were moved to experience more than you normally do, to reach a heightened state of emotion. Something you observed in the characters touched on your own passion and brought it out, if only momentarily.

When this happens to me, I am reminded of the power of my heart. Each time it is a revelation. I see a character make a life choice based on the desires of her heart and realize the truth in her example. She is honest with herself or, to use a much-abused cliché, she is true to her heart. Such vicarious experiences resonate deeply. If only we had the necessary courage, we too would make such choices. Our hearts race, leap, and soar. These little windows into our own hearts, these small moments of exhilaration, show us that our passion, no matter how out of touch, remains vital.

A LIFE WITHOUT REGRET

When we act in opposition to our heart, defying our passion, we are left with feelings of emptiness, longing, and unfulfillment. When we rule out passion, we introduce ourselves to a life of regret, a life of what-ifs. What if I had gone after my dreams? Could I have realized them? What if I had tried to be a musician or an executive or a doctor? What if I could have been good enough? Would I have made it? What if I had had the courage to take that trip, make that move, apply for that job?

Probably you already have asked yourself such questions. If you are like most, at some point you have looked your passion in the face and denied it. If you did, you sold yourself short. You let self-doubt, caution, and fear make decisions for you.

I often hear people muse about regret. On one's deathbed, they say, no one will wish they had spent more time at the office—a modern cliché. I don't think it's that simple. Most of us spend time at work out of necessity. We must provide for ourselves and our families. In retrospect, I think more would wish they had spent more time at a different job, or in the same organization doing things differently. Even parents who stay at home to raise their children might have similar regrets. They might wish they had had more fun with their children or that they had worried less about what parenting books said was important and more about what their children needed.

Passioneers live with few regrets. They learn the lesson that is so hard for many: to achieve and preserve happiness by following your passion, you cannot give up more than you will gain. You must keep your eye on the prize, so to speak. You must know what your Profit is and pursue your passion in a way that leads you toward it rather than away from it. This is where our troubled celebrities usually make their mistake. They decide fame is the end, or living large, or making money. They might consider their families and friends as an afterthought, their health as an aside. Their passion mutates and distorts, often bearing no resemblance to the feeling it originally was. The passioneer on the contrary treats passion thoughtfully, taking great care to protect it and nurture it, realizing that some sacrifice may be necessary to ensure its continued survival.

You have an innate sense of the balance between risk and benefit whether you choose to heed it or not. When you take a job that pays less but offers more room for advancement, you acknowledge that you value certain things more than others, that you are willing to give something up in favor of something else that is more important. When passion is involved, the stakes are often high. If my neighbor discovered that his greatest passion was mountain climbing, I would not advise him to sell his house, abandon his family, buy a sport utility vehicle, and travel from mountain to mountain surviving on trail mix and water. He might (though I doubt it) feel no regret in doing so initially, but he certainly would later when he was out of money, alone, and shunned by his family. A true passioneer would evaluate his life, decide what he wanted to gain from mountain climbing, and find a way to pursue it within the bounds of current reality.

Gibran (1995 [1923], pp. 50–51) acknowledged the potential for contention between the human elements, but also recognized the way of the passioneer as the answer:

> Your reason and your passion are the rudder and the sails of your seafaring soul.
>
> If either your sails or your rudder be broken, you can but toss and drift, or else be held at a standstill in mid-seas.
>
> For reason, ruling alone, is a force confining; and passion, unattended, is a flame that burns to its own destruction.
>
> Therefore let your soul exalt your reason to the height of passion, that it may sing;
>
> And let it direct your passion with reason that your passion may live through its own daily resurrection, and like the phoenix rise above its own ashes.

Your passion can lead you to the heights and achievements you seek when accompanied by the guiding force of reason. The secrets of endurance, renewal, and enthusiasm reside in the marriage of the two. Either alone is wasted.

WHICH PATH WILL YOU FOLLOW?

Figures 1.1 and 1.2 show what can result from the balance you strike between your head and your heart. If you listen only to your heart and passions (path A in Figure 1.1), you are less con-

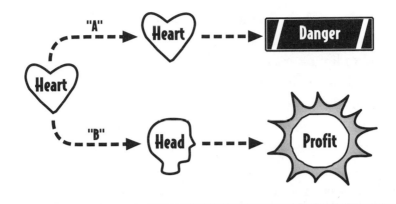

Figure 1.1. Heart-Driven Approaches.

cerned about what you have now and you do not consider the negative directions passion can lead you to. To put it simply, you set yourself up for danger—physical, emotional, or financial. In following your heart you must be willing to make sacrifices, but you do not want to give up anything you will regret losing in the long run. That would leave you unhappier than if you had never pursued your passion. Spouses, once lost, are not easily won back. Money, once thrown away, does not magically reappear.

The second outcome (path B in Figure 1.1) of heart-driven approaches, the one we all dream of, is Profit. It is the result of starting from your heart and then using reason to determine the best outlet for your passion. By doing so you tap into your unique reserves of energy and ability. You evaluate opportunities and plan how to integrate your passion into your life, laying the groundwork for reaching your goals and enriching your life along the way. The key to this approach is to embrace your passion *first* and then use your intelligence and reasoning to nurture, develop, and incorporate it into your life.

Figure 1.2 shows the results of starting with your head. When logic and reason dictate what we hope for, we are bound to limit ourselves. We convince ourselves that Profit is a nice idea but that we must settle for what is practical. We talk ourselves out of taking risks. Friends have told me, "Starting a successful business might be achievable for you, but I do not have enough money, time, or ideas to make it work for me." Usually this is not true. Rather than opening up to their passions—to create, to sell, to achieve, or to excel—they reason them away as impossible or impractical. They render their dreams unattainable.

The irony is these people still cling to their dreams as if they might spontaneously come true. Perhaps a wealthy benefactor will find them out of the blue and provide them with a large cash infusion to get things started. Maybe they will casually mention one of their ideas at a dinner party and be overheard by someone who wants to help them. Maybe they will be "discovered" walking down the street and win instantaneous fame. Not likely! Especially if you do not allow your passion to manifest itself in some way through *action*. Actresses discovered in coffee shops fall out of the limelight quickly if they exude no passion in their acting. Business owners are ousted by directors or sink their enterprises if they lose their fire.

Even beginning with Profit in mind, we may lose the passion that distinguishes our performance and helps us reach our goals. If you are not excited by what you are doing, you are less likely to be a top performer or to win recognition. Not that you cannot do a great job when you start from your head. Determination has gotten many people far in this life. Claims such as "I am going to become a vice president by forty, what-

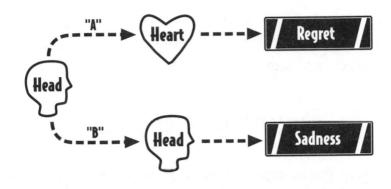

Figure 1.2. Head-Driven Approaches.

ever it takes" often prove true. Unfortunately, those who profess them usually do so at great expense to their heart and in turn to their happiness. Those who start from their heart somehow set themselves apart, which helps them end up where they want to be.

When you start from your head and consider the whisperings of your heart only as an afterthought (path A in Figure 1.2), you choose a life of regret. Every step of the way you make decisions that you know belie your heart. You remain aware of your desires enough to pine for them but not enough to exercise them. People who choose this path often become bitter or sad, wondering what could have been if they had only listened to their heart. When they go to their grave, they take with them a long list of "I wish I would haves."

The other alternative for those who start from their head is to rule out their heart completely (path B in Figure 1.2). Such people end up living in ways that do not resemble who they are or once were inside. They sell their dreams for a mess of pottage—a condo by the ocean, a dull career—whatever they believe to be the prudent life. They are not necessarily cold or unfeeling, but they lack the joy and self-knowledge that comes from being in touch with your heart.

PASSION IS THE CORE OF YOU

Why is all this so important? Because passion is at the core of you—it is who you are. Without it we would be automatons, going through the motions of life without feeling or distinction. Passion gives you life. It defines you just as much as where you come from and who you spend time with. Philosopher Edmund Burke went so far as to declare that passion is "the central part of human character."

Not long ago, I read a modern fable by Pablo Coehlo called *The Alchemist* (1998). The central character learns that the key to his happiness is following his heart. By so doing he will fulfill his personal legend and find his "treasure." According to the story, each of us has a legend that is distinctly ours. Our heart provides us with clues, but most of us ignore them and we therefore fail to live our legend—we let our lives wander in no apparent direction, toward no apparent end. We die, as Oliver Wendell Holmes (1884) observed, with our music still inside us.

Whether you subscribe to the Jungian notion of a collective unconscious, biological theories of instinct and intuition, or religious explanations of the spirit, you must acknowledge that there is a potential for accomplishment in each of us. Passion is a manifestation of that potential. It is the key to unlocking it. If you are like most of us, you find yourself wondering what you are supposed to contribute to the world, what

Passion Review

Passion Benefits
*(positive results of exercising
passion wisely)*

- Self-realization
- Energy, enthusiasm
- Heightened
  performance/experience
- Living without regret

Passion Pitfalls
*(negative results of exercising
passion irresponsibly)*

- Excess, "going off the
  deep end"
- Loss of perspective
- Disregard for reason
- Abandoning the important
  for the exciting

role you are to play in its evolution. Whatever you are doing now, you probably sense that there is something more you could or should be doing. It might be important to millions or only to you, but you must know that the time to begin realizing your potential—whether the result is treasure, happiness, or karma—is now. Now is the time to begin following your heart and living your passion.

Passion Defined

By now you're probably asking, what exactly is passion? To use it, you must understand it. But understanding it poses a challenge, because passion is not simply defined. Webster offers no less than twelve definitions, only some of which pertain here. But there is a common denominator to most: strong emotion. One Webster definition is "any powerful or compelling emotion or feeling." Another is "a strong or extravagant fondness, enthusiasm, or desire for anything." Both are facets of passion that merit further explanation.

The Passion in Everybody

The word passion covers a gamut of intense emotions: love and hate, joy and despair. In this book it is used to describe the underlying force that fuels all these emotions. We all have passion; the choices we make determine how it expresses itself. So I like to describe passion as personal intensity, the special part of our nature that determines what topics or activities stir the powerful emotions in us. If you have a passion for something, it strikes a chord in you. It heightens your awareness, engages your attention, and kindles your excitement. If you betray or defy it, you feel miserable, angry, or confused. But if you fall out of touch with your passion after years of neglecting it, often your feelings will be more muted: you might feel only apathy or a tinge of regret.

If so, you are probably living a dispassionate life. This does not mean you have no happy or sad moments. But in general you are numb to your passion and therefore numb to the world. The environment you create for yourself—the people with whom you surround yourself, the jobs you take, the activities you pursue—do not reflect your passion. They cannot stir the wellspring of emotion that fuels greatness and fulfillment. You are not living with intensity.

Passioneers, however, recognize their passion and welcome it into their life. They crave the rush it gives them and seek to keep it flowing by doing things that feed it. Thus passion directs them and ensures their commitment, perseverance, and performance. They feel more satisfaction and freedom. They are acutely aware of their surroundings and create environments that feed their passion rather than subdue it. They know that they have power, through the choices they make, to actively engage their passion and use it to create an exciting and fulfilling life.

THE PASSION IN YOU

We all share the capacity for personal intensity. Nobody is born without it. But many of us never learn to tap into the source of our intensity because we fail to discover what inspires it: we do not discover our personal passions. *Passion* refers to the force for intensity in all of us; *passions* are the things that elicit—draw out—our passion individually. Your passions might be writing, gardening, and working with children; mine might involve business, competition, and personal improvement. In considering the distinction between the two, think of your life as a building under construction. Your passions are the bricks that give shape to the building, whereas your passion is the mortar that holds it all together. The variety of passions is limitless, so the buildings we construct are as varied as the urban skyline. But few of us are fortunate enough to discover all or even some of our passions, so our buildings remain unfinished—skyscrapers, cathedrals, warehouses, and monuments unrealized.

A friend of mine once dreamed of being an actor. Certainly she was not alone in that dream. But others outgrew

it while she still felt it. She knew she was passionate about acting because whenever she pondered it her heart raced. She
delivered heartfelt soliloquies and powerful performances
before her mirror to an imaginary audience, but she was too
scared to pursue her passion outside the safety of her bedroom.
Indeed, she never acted—not so much because anyone's chance
of becoming a movie star is slim but because she doubted her
passion and was afraid to pursue it. Eventually she lost the feeling and chose to focus on a career as an advertising executive.
Today, as a middle-aged woman, she regrets her cowardice and
finds herself wondering if she could have made it.

     My friend was lucky in one sense: she recognized one of
her passions. That she could not act on it is not unusual. One
purpose of this book is to show you how to live out your passions once you find them. Even more common, and more difficult to address, is the failure to identify your passions at all.
If Beethoven had not been forced to play the piano by his
father while young, would he have discovered his great passion and genius for music? What if he had been born to the
bread makers or chimneysweeps next door? Would his passion ever have manifested itself? Often I wonder what we are
missing. Might we possess a passion for something that we
never encounter? Might we not miss our call to personal greatness? I think the answer is yes. If so, we must actively seek out
our passions in order to make them a central, ruling force in
our lives.

What Passion Is

Chapter Four is devoted to discovering your passion, both
plural and singular. I hope that by showing you ways that oth-

Passion Review

Passion: personal intensity; an underlying force that fuels our strongest emotions

Passions: activities, ideas, and topics that elicit these emotions

ers have done so you may begin your own process of discovery. Now, however, consider some of the characteristics of passion so that you may recognize how it may already be present in your life. First, passion is *natural*. As I have said, passion is part of you. You do not need to create it, only to give it form and function and help it thrive.

Second, passion is *dynamic*. Acknowledge and nurture it, and it will most certainly evolve to encompass new areas and directions. If your passion is for teaching and you spend many years in the classroom, for example, that passion may evolve to include sharing your knowledge of teaching. You might develop teacher training programs, lecture teachers' organizations, or start a television program to promote good teaching techniques. But the core passion stays the same: helping people learn.

As one passion evolves, you may discover others. If, per the last example, you start a TV program or begin lecturing, you might discover that you have a great love for public speaking. That might lead you to seek opportunities you never imagined as a teacher.

Some might argue that passion is limiting because it blinds you or makes you single-minded. Not so! Passioneers find that passion expands their horizon rather than confines it. Passion brings out your best. When we perform well and are pleased with where we are going, we are willing to try more. We are more self-confident and therefore entertain more possibilities for our future. We envision success rather than defeat, progress rather than stagnation. In this way, passion is *empowering*.

Perhaps most important, passion is *unconditional*. It may evolve, but it is unwavering. You may bludgeon it, suppress it, squash it, or lose sight of it, but it is a given, a constant. When you act from your heart, you do not need to call on your reserves for energy or initiative. Your passion is ready and willing to provide all the stamina and inspiration you need. If, for example, you have a passion for sailing and someone offers you an afternoon on a schooner, you could have a fever of 103, a stack of documents to review, or a party to attend, but you'd still get to the dock on time—even if you had to finish the documents in record time, miraculously fight off the fever, or make a circuit of the harbor before the party started. If sailing was that important to you, none of these things would be show stoppers. If not, you might tell yourself that it would be nice to go sailing, but chances are you would procrastinate and lose the opportunity—while still getting behind in other activities.

WHAT PASSION IS NOT

Passion is not an addiction. It is not limiting, nor is it all-consuming. When passion pervades your life, you are instinctively aware of the need for diversity and equilibrium. But if you abandon all else in pursuit of a passion, it becomes an obsession: you cut yourself off from growth and other foundations of happiness. True passion allows no such thing. It thrives in various environments and situations. But pursued relentlessly—in a vacuum, so to speak—it assumes another form or shrivels up entirely. I met a singer who, after giving up his family and friends by traveling from city to city and club to club for more than fifteen years, woke up one morning and realized he did not enjoy singing any more. His passion had become addiction and ended up costing him more than he knew.

I have often heard passion used to justify workaholism. It does not. Ironically, most workaholics I know loathe what they do. They dread waking up in the morning, resent the pervasiveness of work in their life, and see no escape from it. I know a young man who graduated from college with a degree in applied mathematics. He didn't hate math but never really loved it either. At graduation he had little sense of what he wanted to do and so ended up as an actuary for a large insurance company. He yawned when describing his duties, but despite his apparent disdain he often pulled all-nighters to crunch numbers for quarterly reports. He spent long hours at the office, day after day and night after night, doing something he cared nothing about. Was he a workaholic? Possibly. Was passion involved? Definitely not.

Knowing this man, I am sure he was very good at what he did. Probably he was a talented actuary; clearly he was highly skilled at his job. The promotions he received testify to that. But his case shows that talent is not passion, and passion is not talent. Not that those who pursue their talents are not passionate about them. Most probably are. But just because you have a natural ability does not mean you are passionate about it.

I know an internationally acclaimed artist whose works are sold around the world as quickly as they are produced. He is known widely in his field; he is certainly talented and definitely passionate about his art. From the time he could hold a crayon, there was never a doubt in his mind that art had to be a central part of his life. His sister also showed great artistic promise, but she did not enjoy drawing. She sketched when her parents asked, but not otherwise. When her brother lectures on creativity to sold-out audiences around the country today, he mentions her—explaining that she too could have been an accomplished artist and that she chose to exercise her creativity in other ways. In other words, her talent was not her passion.

The opposite is also true: passion does not ensure talent. I see this in a group of street performers observed recently. No doubt many of them strum guitars, bang drums, and wail love songs because they are passionate about their music. But few of them are talented at it. Passion gives us the energy to apply ourselves and work to develop our skills, but it cannot create something from nothing. Every self-help book includes stories of people who have overcome hardship or limitations. But the bottom line is that they could accomplish no more than their physical, intellectual, and emotional capabilities would allow.

Wilma Rudolph is often cited as someone who achieved the impossible. As a girl she suffered from polio, pneumonia, and scarlet fever that left her body shriveled and weakened. She could barely walk when she reached adolescence, so no one expected her to win three Olympic gold medals in track and field and become known as the fastest woman on the planet. Certainly her courage and fortitude were phenomenal. More important, regardless of how her body appeared to the rest of the world, she knew its potential. She sensed that the bones and tissues, when combined with her passion and underlying ability, were capable of greatness.

We cannot look to our passion naïvely or as a panacea for our problems. Humans are born with limitations. My passion for tennis is not going to make me Pete Sampras. But it can be a vital part of my life if, recognizing reality, I choose to coach a kids' team or officiate at the local tennis club. I believe passion can help you transcend barriers that appear to be limitations. We are capable of more than we know, more than we imagine. But passion is not the key to a perfect life.

The street performers I mentioned earlier also illustrate another important aspect of passion: it is not forced. No one compelled them to take to the street to earn money, and I am almost certain no one encouraged them because of their natural ability. I assume most of them are there because they feel they must be. Like my business instincts, their music finds a way out. It literally bursts forth from them. Some do what they do for money, others to bring smiles to people's faces. Whatever their motivation, their passion for their music dwarfs any fear or embarrassment that might keep them from performing.

Street performers are a rare breed. Not the panhandlers who change acts from dancing to singing to magic tricks from week to week, but the true passioneers who, against prudence and better judgment, expose themselves to critics, hecklers, and scoffers just so they can do what they love. On a recent trip to a southern city in the United States I watched an old man tap dancing in a public square. He took the quarters and dollar bills people threw in his top hat, but I think he dances for a deeper reason. He had been dancing, after all, for over sixty years, and surely had had many opportunities to earn a better living. Perhaps he even had a career that kept him in

Passion Review

Passion is . . .	Passion is not . . .
• Natural	• Addiction
• Dynamic	• Talent
• Empowering	• Forced
• Unconditional	• Fleeting

fresh taps and bow ties. Clearly, the joy that filled his eyes when he danced came from passion, and he was living it in the best way he knew how.

He illustrates another important characteristic of passion: it is not fleeting. If you question whether something you enjoy is a passion, a telltale sign is if your energy for it wanes from day to day. As I mentioned, passion may evolve, but it never fizzles. For this man, expressing his passion by dancing day in and day out is a constant source of fulfillment. Perhaps he also pursues it by teaching his art to children or by encouraging his younger colleagues. No matter how he chooses to pursue it, the basic passion remains.

CONTENT-BASED PASSION

Now that you understand more about what passion is and is not, how can you begin to distinguish your passions? The tap dancer's passion is very specific—what I call a content-based passion or a passion that centers on a highly specialized activity. To keep such a passion in our life, we must also keep the activity in our life. Many athletes are driven by content-based passion. Their passion is for their sport, not necessarily for competition. It is expressed only in that sport, not in any other. Ask an all-star basketball player if his athletic passion includes hockey and he may look befuddled. Ask a tennis player if she spends eight hours a day on the court simply so she can beat her competitors and she might answer, "Not exactly."

What motivates athletes such as these is the love of the game, nothing more and nothing less. For example, I know a professional golfer—call her Beatrice. Beatrice stepped onto a golf course for the first time at age fourteen and was immediately hooked. She was energized by the prospect of mastering something that looked so easy but in reality was so hard. She competed on her high school team but, in the absence of scholarships for female golfers, had to pursue her passion on the side in college. After graduation she moved and sought the help of a respected golf pro. She borrowed money to do so and knew she would have to return home, dreams in tow, if she could not find a way to earn a living while working on her game. Fortunately, things fell into place. The pro offered her a part-time job that provided living expenses, and so, almost every day for four and a half years, she practiced her strokes. Her goal was to make it onto the LPGA tour—she had to win money if she wanted to make her passion, golf, into a career.

Every six months for four years she tried to qualify, and every six months she fell short. Finally, she decided her time was up. On her final try, she made it. But then the pressure became even greater. Players are ranked by wins; if she did not win, she could not stay on the tour.

Beatrice qualified for the tour every year for twenty years and earned more than $1.5 million during that time, quitting only because (she told me) her body no longer performed as she would like it to. But she keeps her passion alive by golfing with an over-forty group of friends (who also feel less agile than they used to). Despite her success, she still feels that golf is the hardest thing she's ever done.

For Beatrice, golf was not about money or winning, though both were important to her. It was about her passion for the sport. Many people like Beatrice possess passions that reside wholly in one pursuit. There are as many content-based passions as there are ways to spend time, ranging from ballet to football to model airplanes. When passioneers discover a content-based passion, it often becomes a recreation for them. Sometimes they feel their discovery has come too late to build a career around it, or the passion might not be relevant to other passions guiding their professional life. For example, a pastry passioneer might opt to bake on the side rather than pursue a career as a chef. A passionate swimmer whose body refuses to move quickly through the water may decide to limit her involvement in the sport to laps in the community pool.

This is the distinguishing factor of content-based passions: they revolve around a single subject or activity, but the ways they can be pursued are many.

CONTEXT-BASED PASSION

Context-based passion revolves around a theme rather than a specific topic or activity. This theme may be common to many activities or areas regardless of their content focus. Some examples of context-based passion are helping, competing, and creating.

To help you understand the difference between content-based and context-based passion, consider this example. Two young executives lead similar companies that design and manufacture computer hardware. Both are praised for the job they do, and both are viewed as integral to their company's success. One has been a computer nut since childhood. She used her allowance to buy her first computer in junior high school and has been attached to a keyboard ever since. She is passionate about technology and is devoted to advancing both the art and the science of computing . . . her "content" focus.

Her counterpart at the company's rival organization also wants to create the best computer possible. While earning his MBA, he learned the value of good product design and its importance in creating a successful business. Above all he is passionate about creating a company. Better computers mean higher profits, and higher profits mean future growth. He enjoys computers and uses them extensively, but he would be equally happy at the helm of a start-up soft drink or auto parts company. His passion relies not on the specifics and "content" of any one product, but rather on the general theme of "creating" a business. His passion stems from context, not content.

Helping others is a context-based passion for many, which translates easily into a number of professions: social work, teaching, nursing, and customer service, for example. Beyond career applications, it might involve volunteer work, coaching, or merely raking an elderly neighbor's leaves. One with a passion for helping might teach English to immigrants without loving the language. Or run recreational programs for the elderly without caring much about games. Or fix meals at the homeless shelter without passion for cooking. What counts to such people is helping others, whatever form it takes.

I am driven by many context-based passions: creating businesses, personal and organizational improvement, learning, competing, and teaching. One of my strongest passions is to achieve personal excellence, and it led me to write this book. I apply this passion in every aspect of my life; I strive to do my best and accomplish as much as I can. Thus I have been competitive in many sports: tennis, water polo, swimming, roller skating, baseball, football, and volleyball. I began bowling in high school, was a college champion, and then joined the pro tour while in graduate school. The money I won helped pay the tuition bills. More importantly, I loved seeing how far I could go and how well I could compete.

If you had asked me at the time whether bowling was a passion for me, I might have answered in the affirmative. But when I look back now, I realize it was not a passion for me. When I completed school, I had plenty of opportunities to grow, and I dropped bowling. I cannot remember the last time I picked up a bowling ball, and my life is no less fulfilling because of it.

To help you identify some of your own context- and content-based passions, the passion review on page 29 (though not comprehensive) gives you additional examples of each.

THREADS OF PASSION

I have always had a passion for achievement. As a student I expressed it through academics, athletics, student government, and music. As a professional I have exercised it by

Passion Review

Content-Based Passions (center on a highly specialized topic)	Context-Based Passions (center on a theme that can apply to one activity or several activities or topics)
• Fishing	• Learning
• Painting	• Competition
• Swimming	• Improvement
• Tennis	• Entrepreneurship
• Chess	• Helping others
• Computers	• Involvement
• Cooking	• Leading

building and growing a business, leading organizations and professional associations, and earning the respect of my colleagues. My passion has been a thread weaving through my life, into and out of activities, across experiences, and through the years. We all have such threads of passion, and they remain with us, sometimes on the surface and sometimes woven deep in our fabric, waiting to reemerge at a later date. Passioneers capture these threads over time and use them to create beautiful designs. Others allow them to become torn or frayed or lose sight of them altogether.

To make passion a defining factor in your life, find your threads and weave them wisely. Decide when to use one and when to put one aside for safekeeping. Grace, a friend of mine, has a passion for reading. Sometimes it has been a guiding pursuit for her, sometimes a minor avocation. Not that her interest in reading ever varies, but sometimes necessity intervenes. Then she builds up "passion reserves," which she unleashes as soon as she can.

Grace attended an Ivy League university and graduated with highest honors. And though she had selected a history major because it involved lots of reading, it was not the type she enjoyed. She didn't care, she told me, to read about "old men in their cobweb-filled offices criticizing Alexander the Great's military maneuvers." When school was in session she squeezed in a novel here and there, but she had little opportunity to indulge pleasure reading.

When summer rolled around, however, Grace rushed to the discount bookseller and stocked up. She became a reading machine. She had a full-time job and full-time boyfriend but always found time for reading. After graduation, Grace married and became an enthusiastic but exhausted mother who read less and less. After her second child was born, she was barely able to glimpse at a newspaper every few days. "I would pick up a book," she said, "and, invariably, as soon as I sat down, someone would need me. And it wasn't just the kids. My husband was a culprit too!"

Once her younger child entered preschool, Grace had some spare time each day. She resumed reading. Indeed, her passion kicked into overdrive. Even balancing motherhood with part-time work, she devoured so many books that her husband, also an avid reader, became envious.

Grace has had a third child now—she is also passionate about being a mother—and no doubt reading once again takes a backseat to parenting. She predicts that the kids' teenage years will similarly impede her passion for reading.

She says so happily and without remorse, because reading is a thread that she can weave into and out of her life as conditions dictate.

PEOPLE OF MANY PASSIONS

As with Grace, our lives are a fabric sewn from many threads. When she became a wife, she brought in a new thread of passion, her love for her husband. When she became a mother, she added the threads of teaching and nurturing her children. In her professional life, she became an accomplished writer. She tells me that writing, though not a passion, leads her to discover new things about herself and therefore feeds her passion for self-awareness. At any given moment in Grace's life, she is following different passions in different ways. The key to her happiness has been her ability to weave all these threads of passion in and out of her life as it changed.

We are people of many passions, both the content-based and context-based forms. We do not express one to the exclusion of the others, although often one gains special significance for us. We are capable of pursuing our passions simultaneously, sequentially, or selectively—whichever best suits our personality. By expressing multiple passions variously as life changes, we ensure that our zest for living remains.

Passion Begets Passion

I did not mention that Grace was able, with the luxury of a double stroller, to take up walking even as the mother of toddlers. Pushing reading into the background for awhile left her room for new pursuits. On her frequent walks, she was exposed to a world she had previously ignored. Her children were lulled to sleep by the passing scenery, but she was invigorated by it. She marveled at the foliage and was even more fascinated by the details of the buildings she observed. Her fancy evolved into a true love of architecture, and now that her children are older, she has taken classes on the history and theory of architecture. She is also building a library of design and architecture books, a perfect way to express both her passions, old and new.

When we let passion into our life, we become resourceful. We begin to find ways to keep it there. We may find new passions when established ones are threatened or use old ones to sustain us through times of trouble. Grace's experience taught her what many of us fail to learn: passion begets passion. Open yourself to one passion and you open the floodgates to many. Passion can be a lifestyle, and passioneers know it. They are painfully aware when passion leaves their lives, and they seek to keep it constant.

The Power of Passion

Paris, another friend of mine, learned firsthand the power of passion when she was a newlywed fresh out of college. She had a whirlwind romance in her last semester. She fell head over heels for the guy down the hall and, immediately after graduating, packed up her diploma and headed to his hometown. Her previous plan to attend law school seemed silly. She found herself wondering how she ever thought that three more years of hiding her head in books could make her happy. What she wanted now was to marry this man—he had already proposed!—and build a life around the excitement she felt with him.

So they married—and then returned to the university, where her husband faced two more years of study. Unsure what she wanted professionally and needing a job yesterday, Paris turned again to law, taking a job as a paralegal. It was a choice of convenience, but also a radical offense against her heart. She was euphoric in her marriage but miserable at work. Her job was tedious and uninspiring. Normally she went after what she wanted, but now Paris accepted that eight hours of her day were not her own until her husband graduated. Then, together, they could decide what they wanted professionally.

But as she drowned in monotony at the office, Paris became miserable. She would get home around eight after working several hours of overtime and collapse. Boredom and sadness exhausted her. To keep her sanity something had to change. But what? She had a husband to support, bills to pay. With only nine more months until her husband graduated, where could she go? No one would pay to train her and then watch her leave so soon. Plus she still didn't know what kind of career she wanted.

Then one day it occurred to her: school. She had always loved school; she had considered law school mainly because it would let her keep learning. She found a state university with a low-tuition evening master's degree program, went for it, and was accepted. She began studying TESOL (teaching English to speakers of other languages) because she and her husband hoped to spend some time in Japan, where the degree could prove lucrative. What she was studying, however, was not as important as the fact that she was studying.

She was learning once again, and loving it! Immediately her paralegal work became more bearable, and a raise in pay kept her from needing to work overtime, which freed her to take a full class load at her new school. And she arrived home late at night energized, not drained.

Paris completed the master's program in nine months but never completed her thesis. She still laughs about that because the degree was not as important to her as passion. When she embraced it, she was no longer trapped. She still had to be practical, but her life became her own and she chose to fill it with passion. Once she did, she could make the most of an otherwise difficult situation.

With passion in her life, Paris's work performance improved even though she didn't like her job. Passion changed her mood and allowed her to focus on the job not as a waste of time but as a constructive means to an end. She actually began to enjoy her time at the office.

Paris experienced what University of Chicago psychology professor Mihaly Csikszentmihalyi (1991, 1997) has termed *flow*, a heightened state of experience during which we become so absorbed in our activities that we lose all sense of time. When we act from passion, when it is a presence in our lives, we flow. We become active participants in life rather than passive observers. We perform better by others' estimations and become happier on our own. We surprise even ourselves when we realize all we have accomplished.

I know you have had a flow experience at some point in your life. There has been a time when you lost yourself completely in an activity, perhaps when writing a paper in college, singing a song, building a birdhouse, reading a book, or playing a sport. When athletes flow they claim to be "in a zone."

Passioneers live their lives in the "passion zone." By keeping the level of passion in their lives high, they also keep their energy level and the quality of their experience high. Passion not only gives the boost we need to flow, it helps us challenge our limitations. Under its influence, we can do things reality dictates we should not. For example, dyslexics learn far more effectively when what they read greatly interests them—when it touches a thread of passion. This seems obvious, right? Wouldn't you do better if you care about what you read? For a twelve-year-old boy comic books are far more engaging than instruction manuals for kitchen appliances, and stories about pirates or spaceships are considerably more interesting than poems about flowers.

So why do we not live as if life were of great interest to us? Why do we not get engaged in things that really get us going? We should, of course. And therein lies the secret of the passioneer.

CONSIDER YOURSELF LUCKY

I interviewed many passioneers for this book, and a common theme surfaced: most consider themselves lucky. Ironically, luck has little to do with it. We choose how to live life. Chance is less a factor than exuberance and industry. Several passioneers I spoke with said they had made difficult changes and weren't sure what to do next but then were called to a great opportunity. The call usually came from people who had heard of them and wanted to tap into their enthusiasm and commitment. This is not luck. This is passion in action. You can begin your own personal transformation in the same way. Consider yourself lucky that you have the opportunity to discover your passion and to make it a part of your life. Then, as your life begins to reflect your passion, know that you have created your own luck. And know that your heart has provided you with answers your head could not.

PASSION INTEGRATION

When you make choices that let passion in and keep it there, you achieve what I call *passion integration,* in which your life becomes a reflection of your heart. Every aspect of your life— your work, your family, your leisure—somehow mirrors what is important to you. Though you may not be excited every moment of every day (even the strongest of passioneers would be hard-pressed to achieve this), the activities you engage in, the places you go, and the people you see bring out your passion and keep it flowing. In this way, your experiences become more meaningful and you profit from them. This profit may take many forms depending on where your passions lie. It might be increased happiness, accomplishment, or freedom. Whatever the goals you work toward, the underlying effect is the same: continuous passion intensifies and enhances the quality of your day-to-day life.

One key to achieving this enrichment, and a practice of the passioneer, is to view your life as comprehensive rather than compartmentalized. Your life is a continuum of experiences, a complex rubric of events and emotions that feed one into another. In some way each experience reflects something about you, something from within you. But when we divide life into areas, viewing experiences at home and work as somehow different and experiences with our children and our friends as categorically distinct, passion may leave us.

Let me explain further. If you decide that your family is the most important consideration in your life, work becomes a secondary pursuit by default. You may view your job as a means to an end—providing for your family. With this attitude, you are likely to work begrudgingly or halfheartedly. You might end up in a profession you are good at but don't really care about because, in your mind, it is distinct and separate from who you really are and what you really care about. What are the chances you will find or create a work environment that reflects your passion? What is the likelihood that your job will be enriching or invigorating? Chances are you will spend many hours each workday in a setting where your passion is stifled or unwelcome and then return home too tired or frustrated to enjoy time with your family. In this way, you shut out even that which you really are passionate about!

You cannot categorize your feelings under work, home, and leisure, so why should you categorize your experiences? Certainly they occur in one of these domains, but they are not and should not be distinct from who you are at the core. To remain close to your passion you need to make it a vital and ever-present part of life. Seek environments and experiences that call it up rather than force it down. Create opportunities for your passions to enter your life in every area, at every chance, and then work to keep them there.

In acknowledgment of this principle, passioneers often have life missions rather than careers. The work they do at any time reflects something about their personality, something they are committed to, something they always want to be learning or doing. They think about this mission in the office, at home, and on vacation. It never leaves them. A passioneer who is a chemist may leave his beakers and flasks in the lab, but experiments and elements are part of his thinking at all times. His passion for chemistry helps shape his view of the world and his place in it. It is a part of him that cannot be turned off no matter where he is.

This does not mean that our chemist is ruled by his job. Far from it. His job is an extension of his passion, not the definition of it. The job—paperwork, logistics, breaks by the water cooler—he can walk away from, his passion he cannot. When he takes a trip with his family—his passion remains with him—not as a list of things to do but as an enthusiasm that will not leave his heart. He is inspired with vision and excited about possibilities. He is tuned in to his world and aware of the opportunities it offers.

His passion for the people in his life is also an integral part of this life mission. His children do not leave his thoughts when he is in the lab. In fact, they account for his presence there just as much as his passion for chemistry. Perhaps he views the work as a legacy to leave them, or a means of bettering the world they are growing up in, or a way to help them appreciate the inherent beauty of the universe. Whatever his motivation, you can be sure that he shares his passion with his family and that they are deeply connected to it. His work is not just a job and neither is his family. They are both necessary and welcome elements in his life, part of a passion continuum.

I want you to experience passion integration. I want you to know that life can be exciting every day and not just on special occasions. I want you to feel the power of passion and realize your potential for personal success. You do not need to be rich, famous, or brilliant to reap the rewards that passion can bring. You only need to be willing to listen and ready to feel.

In the next chapter, I introduce the Passion Plan and show how you can bring passion into your life and keep it there. By following the plan you reacquaint yourself with your heart and discover the passions, both content- and context-based, that define you and hold the key to building the life you want to live. You will learn how to use passion in conjunction with reason to improve performance, heighten experience, and realize your Profit.

ARE YOU READY FOR PASSION?

If you question where you stand with regard to passion, answer the following questions. If you doubt that passion can help you or that you lack it, you might be surprised by what your answers reveal.

Passion Readiness Evaluation

1. Do you lack motivation and excitement when going about daily activities?

2. Do you dream of doing something different with your life?

3. Do you spend a lot of time doing things you don't want to do?

4. Do you wish you had more time to do the things you love?

5. Do you routinely relegate the activities you enjoy most to lowest priority?

6. Have you forgotten or fallen away from the things that excite you?

7. Have you chosen your current lifestyle (job, housing, and hobbies) because it is safe or practical?

8. Do you feel you are capable of more than you are currently achieving?

9. Have you reached your current success at the expense of your happiness? Do you regret decisions you have made along the way?

10. Do you want to love your life?

If you answered yes to any of these questions, then you are ready for the Passion Plan. Read on and learn how to discover your passion, to develop it, to live the life you will love.

CHAPTER 2

From Passion to Profit
A Model for Success

I think that what we're seeking is an experience of being alive, so that our life experiences on the purely physical plane will have resonance with our innermost being and reality, so that we actually feel the rapture of being alive.

JOSEPH CAMPBELL, *THE POWER OF MYTH*, 1988

Letting passion into your life is a personal revelation. Keeping it there is a grand achievement. Using it to lead you to your dreams is the work of a lifetime. And what a wonderful and powerful work it is! I want to help you get in touch with the passion that defines you so you too can have an amazing life. I want you to find what is in your heart and let it enrich your experience. I want you to show the world all you are capable of, all that deep down you know you can be. But most important, I want you to be happy. I want you to live every day with zest and vigor. I want you to love your life.

So let's get down to business. How can you begin to work these wonders today? What changes can you make that will bring out your best and make you thrilled to be alive? How are you going to become a passioneer?

Begin with passion. There is no alternative. No matter how great your accomplishments in the eyes of the world, if you do not begin with passion you will not be happy. Content, maybe. Happy, no. Your life must be a reflection of the desires of your heart if you are to live with exhilaration and without regret. Anything less, anything different, breeds unhappiness. How else could it be that we live among so many who have so much—money, respect, fame, accolades—but who are still secretly miserable?

Passion is not enough, though. It is too powerful a force to let it flow unchecked. Giving over to it completely rarely results in the ends we desire. This is why the Passion Plan is so important. Before you blaze your own passion trail, you need to devote serious time and energy to deciding how you want passion to change your life.

THE PASSION PLAN

The plan begins with passion and leads to Profit. As you might remember, Profit with a capital P is the culmination of your dreams, the results you seek in building a better life. It reflects your greatest goals and deepest desires. It might be measured in dollars, but more likely in terms of experiences and emotions. Profit is what you want most in life.

Along the path to Profit are seven steps you must take to ensure that your passion leads to your desired outcomes (see Figure 2.1). Each is equally important in building a passion-

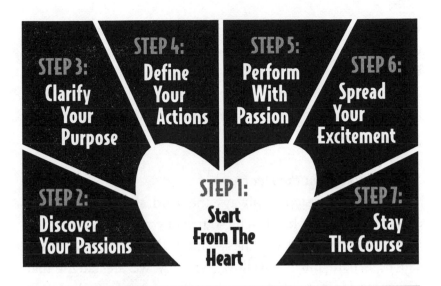

Figure 2.1. The Passion Plan Model.™

filled life and in getting the results you seek. If any one is lacking, reaching your Profit becomes difficult, if not impossible. Because all the steps are critical, a chapter is devoted to each. Here, however, I introduce you to them and show how they work together. The steps come in three phases that reflect the sources from which your change will stem: feeling, thinking, and acting.

Feeling

The first two steps in the plan—start from the heart and discover your passions—require you to get in touch with your heart, to identify your dreams and passions. This is the key to passioneering: feeling first. Your heart will reveal what really matters to you and what brings you happiness. Start from any other source and you set yourself up for frustration and regret. Fulfillment comes only when the results you seek and the activities you embrace are in accordance with the person you are. You cannot look to reason or judgment for insights into your soul. Who you are is what's in your heart.

Step 1: Start from the Heart

Taking the first step is always the hardest. Admitting and accepting that your heart—the source of your greatest strength but also your greatest weakness—holds the key to a better life can be a hard pill to swallow. Typically we are taught that power resides in intellect, not emotion. To start from the heart, we must overcome prejudice against our emotions and desires and recognize the power they provide. We need to move beyond self-imposed limitations, such as fear, doubt, and uncertainty, and embrace our potential.

Step 2: Discover Your Passions

This includes getting in touch with the things that inspire passion in you and recognizing the feeling that accompanies them. Discovery is a gradual process that can involve uncovering lost or forgotten passions, discovering completely new passions, or pinpointing the passions you presently feel but do not understand. It requires you to confront your weaknesses and to find the courage to let passion begin to work in your life.

Whatever your stage of life, you have probably lost touch with some or all of your passions. As children we are ruled by passion. We know little fear and try whatever moves us at the moment. We are passionate about our favorite friends, hobbies, and music groups. With the onset of adulthood, however, we often convince ourselves that passion is childish and impractical. Those who cling to passion into our adult years usually find it necessary to temper it to better reflect the realities of day-to-day existence. We become like birds with clipped wings, aware of our past ability to fly but unable to do it any longer. Regardless of how deep your passion is buried, you can rediscover it.

If you have *never* identified your passions, you need to open yourself to opportunities and experiences that can put you in touch with them. Reading books, taking classes, talking with friends, and trying new activities all serve this end. If you have an inkling or even a strong sense of what things move you, take the time to identify them more specifically. You might, for example, love the time you spend working out at the gym with your friends. But what exactly brings out this emotion in you? Is it the rush of pushing yourself physically, the euphoria generated by the loud music, the camaraderie with your friends, or a pure love of exercise? By examining your experiences and the feelings they stir, you can begin to put a name to your passions. Then, and only then, can you begin to use them to build a better life.

Thinking

After you come to terms with your heart, it is time for reasoning and rationalizing. Steps Three and Four—clarify your purpose and define your actions—require you to think. Because the world can dissuade us from pursuing our passions, we must pursue them with forethought and care. The mind provides us with a formidable defense against threats to passion.

Your intellect can help you define a purpose and set a strategy for following your heart. It can help you determine the most effective ways to integrate passion into your life and ensure that it stays there.

Step 3: Clarify Your Purpose

Once you discover and define your passions, clarify where you want them to lead you. What is your purpose? Do you seek fame and fortune, personal growth and enrichment, world peace and harmony? The purpose you define will determine how you follow your passions. It provides the rationale and the context for carrying them out.

As mentioned, I discovered while very young a passion for creating and building businesses. There were limitless ways to pursue that. Should I open a restaurant, design and market my own line of clothing, sell stocks, build houses? I considered many options, but eventually realized that I was most passionate about excellence and helping others. So I began working in the world of consulting, helping others make personal and organizational improvements. My purpose thus became twofold: to achieve my potential as an entrepreneur and to assist others in achieving their potential. Creating a consulting firm seemed the perfect medium for carrying out not one but many of my passions.

Other purposes were served in building my business, but they were ancillary. One was to make money; without it, the business would not survive and I could not continue living out my passion through it. Another was to increase my interpersonal skills. Still another was to create an organization that provides the opportunity for others to express their passions. There were many more, but those I assigned as most important became the defining factors in carrying out my passions.

Purpose stems from passion, but it is a step removed. Passion is part of you; purpose you create. It may be a natural extension of passion or it may emanate from reason. If you have a passion for working with people, your purpose in pursuing it might be to earn a living, build self-worth, uplift others, or make the world better. Depending on your focus, you could pursue your passion professionally as a counselor, in your spare time as a volunteer, or at home as a parent.

This is not to say you cannot have more than one purpose. On the contrary, you can and should have many. Perhaps you feel an overriding reason for your existence, whether to serve others, advance science, or raise good children. This purpose is your life mission. You might then acknowledge many peripheral purposes that relate to various areas of your life. But no matter how many purposes you have, they all in some way reflect your heart. They justify your passion and bring significance to pursuing it.

Step 4: Define Your Actions

After clarifying your purpose, define the actions to take to achieve it by creating an action plan. You may think passion defies planning, that it is free and spontaneous, but not so. Passion is powerful, but for it to thrive and endure it needs structure. You can and must bolster the power of passion by planning its growth.

Your action plan can, in fact must, include many aspects of your life or career. It is not a series of steps to follow one by one but a blueprint for addressing many areas simultaneously. Suppose, for example, you read this book and realize that your greatest passion is physical fitness. No surprise: you are a regular at the health club and carefully watch what you eat. Surprise: you want to change the purpose that fitness plays in your life. Maybe you even want to make a career change based on it. But how?

Generally your first move would not be to quit your job and live on a regimented fitness diet. That is too drastic and certainly unwarranted. You might begin by learning more about fitness-related fields. You might ask a trainer at the gym how she got involved. You might organize fitness outings for your friends. You might decide you know enough to write your own book on the topic. Once you open your mind to the possibilities, you will be amazed how many there are. And they are probably well within reach.

By developing an action plan that accounts for timing and opportunity, you can make changes confident that you understand the old but are prepared for the new. You can integrate passion into your life at a pace and intensity you can handle. Though you may feel intimidated or discouraged when implementing your plan, you will be prepared to face these challenges, secure in the knowledge that your actions are in concert with your passions and are important steps in reaching your Profit.

Acting

Once you have felt and thought, it is time to act. Equipped with both your passions and your plans, you are ready to go for it! You will, of course, begin to make changes in your life. As you do, you continue to use both heart and head to make decisions; your task is to understand both intimately so that your choices further you on your road to Profit. How you act will determine whether you remain in an active state of pursuit or slip back into a passive state of wishing or worrying.

Step 5: Perform with Passion

Once you have a plan, you must implement it. This element of the Passion Plan puts your passion to the test. You can discover, identify, focus, and plan, but all these are in vain unless you actually integrate your passion into your life.

The first step is, again, the hardest. Probably you will have to leave your comfort zone and take risks. The stakes differ, but the payoff is the same: living your passion becomes easier. You might have to overcome fear, sacrifice financial security, or lay your pride on the line, but once you do you will begin to enjoy experiences more and feel empowered to make choices that will change your life for the better.

When you perform with passion, you view the world in terms of opportunities rather than obstacles and abilities rather than limitations. You see the power of passion firsthand and understand why it is a vital force for change and growth. You begin to create success on your own terms. In short, you become a passioneer.

Step 6: Spread Your Excitement

As passion predominates in your life, you change and others notice. You seem energized, directed, and empowered. You have the confidence and composure of those who actively pursue happiness. In other words, your passion shows. Rather than quietly accept compliments or recognition, use the attention to feed your passion and make it grow.

The key is to share your passion. If you are excited, you can help excite others. Then they share your energy and increase your chances of success. This is true whether you want to distinguish yourself at work, build harmony in your home, or gain skill at a hobby. Through the persuasiveness of your passion you can enlist others to help achieve your goals.

Also, sharing passion models it for your friends, family, and coworkers and gives them a living example of how passion can improve their lives. Under your influence, they might share your passion, but their excitement may only be temporary. As they become acquainted with your passion, they might also discover their own. This makes you a missionary of sorts, a messenger of the heart—a passionary. Respect and value this role: not only will you inspire others but you will be strengthened by the passion they return.

Step 7: Stay the Course

Finally, you must *stay the course,* or persist. Reaching your Profit will probably require a long-term plan. The road to success may not be quick and probably won't be easy. Your passion may dwindle as you face obstacles and unexpected circumstances. If it does, reach within yourself and find the strength to endure.

Passion or no passion, we like to make excuses. We abandon a diet because it was ineffective. We scrap our New Year's resolutions because we were overly optimistic when we made them. We give up on our dreams because they were foolish to begin with. There is always an excuse, a reason, a rationalization for abandoning our goals.

The hardest thing about the Passion Plan, perhaps, is to stick with it. But passion gives you a unique and powerful advantage: your heart is in it. The challenge is to enlist your mind and will to follow. You need to be committed to your passion for the long haul, because although things might fall into place for you, they might not.

However passionate you may be, you will encounter hurdles. When that happens, return to your passion for renewal and strength. It will provide the energy and stamina you need to reach your goal.

A Return to Profit

If you remain true to your passion and follow these seven steps, you *will* find the results you seek. And you will reap rewards you never anticipated, because passion can take you to another level of living. It can open worlds and expand horizons. It can bring new awareness and heightened perceptions. It can empower and improve.

Your idea of Profit may change as you begin to fulfill your potential. The Profit you find might include new passions or new experiences. Whatever its nature, it will further fuel your passion and propel you to even greater achievement and happiness.

YOUR PASSION PLAN

The rest of this book examines the Passion Plan step by step. Worksheets help you focus on each step. Use them to shape your ideas and explore the possibilities for using passion in your life. When you complete each, the result is your personal Passion Plan, a document that captures your passion and creates a vision for following it. Review the worksheets briefly to see how together they can prepare you to feel, think, and act on your passion.

The steps covered in the next seven chapters are these:

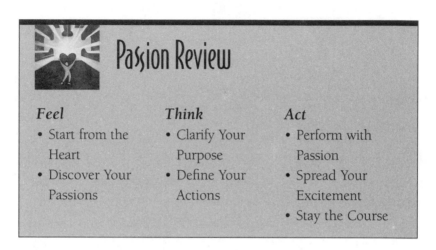

Passion Review

Feel	*Think*	*Act*
• Start from the Heart	• Clarify Your Purpose	• Perform with Passion
• Discover Your Passions	• Define Your Actions	• Spread Your Excitement
		• Stay the Course

CHAPTER 3

Step One
Start from the Heart

For where your treasure is, there will your heart be also.

MATTHEW 6:21

D o you live with passion? Is lack of passion really your problem? In this chapter, I will define the symptoms of passion deficit to help you determine whether you are a candidate for the Passion Plan. I will also show you how to defy the forces that keep passion out of your life and how to welcome it back in.

Possibly you are already passion centered, but the mere fact that you are reading this book suggests that something is missing, that you long for something that passion can offer you. As you read on, try to listen to your heart. It will tell you if you are in the right place, if this is what you need.

PASSION DEFICIT

Those without passion are at a disadvantage to those who possess it; they cannot easily focus, enjoy, be who they really are.

Without the energy and vitality passion provides, we fall into what I call *passion deficit,* the symptoms of which are all too common. In my work with individuals and organizations I have learned that passion deficit is the status quo, not the exception. People everywhere have come to believe that boredom, frustration, fatigue, and stress are the necessary byproducts of modern life. Most of them, in a word, are unhappy. There are myriad reasons for this, but our explanations are usually similar: my job is awful, my spouse doesn't understand me, my kids don't listen to me. . . ." This is the first and most glaring symptom of passion deficit: blaming your unhappiness on others. When passion is part of your life, you create your own happiness. You do not need to blame others for your moods; your energy and fulfillment come from within.

Even if you do not feel unhappy, you may think something is missing in your life. This is a second symptom of passion deficit: longing. When passion is absent or suppressed, you are left with a deep sense of yearning. You might not know what you desire, but you know something is absent, that somehow and somewhere you should be doing more. Longing may express itself in many emotions: sadness, anger, and regret, to name a few.

Many of the passioneers interviewed for this book told me about their longings. Surprisingly, they described it not as a negative or a source of unhappiness but as an agent of change. More than a few described it as an itch—an irrepressible longing for change when life strays out of accordance with passion. You may feel just such an itch but be reluctant to make the changes necessary to scratch it. In the case of one passioneer, then an architect, scratching his itch meant leaving a successful practice to find work that was more fulfilling, or, as he put it, "more fun." For another it was restructuring her free time to accommodate her itch to write novels.

Sometimes a passion deficit surfaces not as a sense of something missing but as a sense that something is wrong. You probably have experienced this at least once: something is out of synch, some element of your life is uncomfortable. Maybe you work in a field you dislike or for an organization that stifles you. Perhaps you are in a bad relationship or in need of a relationship—hopefully a good one. Or it could be a spiritual matter; maybe you are disillusioned with your church or disappointed with the level of your faith. Often we do not understand these feelings and therefore do not strive to correct the situation. Passioneers, however, are in tune with their heart and instructed by it. They recognize what things inhibit their passions and work to eliminate them.

Those who cannot are left with a hodgepodge of emotions that alienate them from their passions and may become confused, frustrated, or even depressed, perhaps incapable of making changes or even doubting the possibility. Many of the people I have counseled have described the effects of these feelings. Some dread getting up in the morning, afraid to face people, jobs, and routines that dishearten them. Others are apathetic, almost devoid of emotion, and find nothing in their day to either inspire or dispirit them. Others feel completely out of control, ruled by tasks and obligations, and devote little or no time to meeting their emotional needs.

If you share any of these feelings, you have probably compromised your passion somewhere along the road. Your life might be far removed, in spirit and in practice, from what your heart craves. But passion deficit does not necessarily result in this feeling. Day to day you might consider yourself happy even though passion is to some degree lacking in your life. Perhaps you engage in activities that elicit your passions and feel you are pursuing them as best you can at the moment. This might be true if you are in school, in the early stages of a new career, building a family, or preparing to retire. Still, whatever point you are at—whether you have reached a milestone or are simply living from one week to the next—you can increase the intensity of your experience and the level of your fulfillment by integrating passion more completely into your life. Passion can help you become a better employee, a better parent, a better boss, a better you. It can bring the excitement, energy, and initiative you need to accomplish your dreams and the peace of mind you need to do so with joy and without regret.

If, despite all this, you are uncertain whether passion is lacking in your life, I want you to remember a time in your life when you were thrilled to be alive, when you were exuberant, enthralled, and exhilarated. For most of us this occurs in youth, when we are feeling our oats in high school, experiencing the rush of freedom in college, or falling prey to the abandon of young love. Or perhaps it happened in adulthood when you reveled in a dream vacation or relished the adventure of beginning a new job. Whenever it was, you are bound to have felt the rush of enthusiasm that accompanies passion and to have sustained it for a time. I am telling you now that you can have that passion back. You may not be able to conjure the identical circumstances that created it or the exact feelings it inspired, but you can regain the same vitalizing energy. You can make passion a salient and compelling force in your life and indulge in the joy that accompanies it.

Passion Review

Symptoms of Passion Deficit
- Blaming others for your unhappiness
- Longing—the feeling that something is missing
- Sadness, anger, or regret
- The feeling that something is wrong or out of synch
- Confusion, frustration, or depression
- Doubting or fearing your ability to change your life

Are you as happy as you should be, as you deserve to be? Are you comfortable with who you are and what you are doing? Do you have a feeling that something should be different? Do you want to be better? Do you crave greater intensity in your life? If your answer is yes to any of these questions, then the Passion Plan is for you. Whether you are young or old, rich or poor, confident or insecure, brazen or timid, you can open your life to passion and rediscover the excitement and empowerment it occasions.

WHERE HAS THE PASSION GONE?

I often wonder how we get so out of touch with our passion, how we get divorced from our heart. Then I glance at a newspaper or take a walk through my neighborhood and the reasons scream out at me. The world seems to conspire against our passion, first draining it from us and then preventing it from coming back.

Ask anyone if there are enough hours in the day and the answer will be an emphatic no. We simply have too much to do and too little time to do it—both at work and at home. And the demands increase even as the satisfaction we derive from our activities decreases. We can never truly relax. We worry about what's next, what we're not getting done, rather than focus on what we could be doing now.

Technology only adds insult to injury. There was a time when offices really closed at 5 P.M., shopping was restricted to malls and markets, phones rang unanswered, and mail was carried only by postal workers. Now our computers, "time-saving" devices that they are, follow us home in stylish leather bags. Our pockets ooze pagers and cell phones, Palm Pilots and day planners. E-mail arrives at all hours and in all places. Shopping and chatting can take place via the Internet long after we should be asleep and resting up for tomorrow's mayhem. And, wouldn't you know, the FedEx man not only rings twice but arrives before 8 in the morning. We can do almost anything anytime. There are no limits on when work ends and personal time begins. The distinction between what we do for others and what we do for ourselves has blurred. It becomes a feat of epic proportions if we actually find an opportunity to reflect on our feelings or gain self-knowledge.

Even when we're not working or fulfilling our responsibilities to others—when we truly have personal time—we are so burned out that we watch TV or find other meaningless tasks instead of actively pursuing something that really moves us. A recent Time/CNN poll cited in the business magazine *Fast Company* (Warshaw, 1998, p. 156) indicated that 65 percent of us spend our leisure time doing things we'd rather not!

How can this be when we have more opportunities and outlets than ever for pursuing our interests?

I believe one reason is that we are not even sure where our interests lie anymore. A friend of mine is a college professor who informally serves as a career counselor and life coach for his students. Every year, he says, more and more students come to him for advice. Because he has gained national recognition in his field, they assume he can guide them to similar success. When they ask him what to do after graduation, he always asks first what they are passionate about. Few have an answer. They just don't know. He attributes this to the sheer volume of information that bombards them daily. Considering the hours we spend each day reading newspapers, watching TV, sifting through mail, and perusing Web sites, it is surprising we ever manage to have a thought of our own. Kids growing up today are enamored of information but also paralyzed by it. The whisperings of their heart are drowned out by the noise of the world.

Adults are no different. We have become numb. A poll conducted by the *Wall Street Journal* and ABC News revealed that 50 percent of Americans would pursue a different profession given the opportunity (Warshaw, 1998, p. 142). I marvel at that. What opportunity are we waiting for? I believe many of us have no clue where to begin or what to look for. We wouldn't recognize opportunity if it bit us on the nose, because we are out of touch with our heart. We simply do not know what we would most like to be doing. We dream of financial freedom, career satisfaction, and a happy family, but we do not know how to get them.

For those unfulfilled in professional life and perhaps even in personal life, such self-limiting behavior only fuels the cycle of stagnation. Rather than challenging our abilities, we tend them like carefully manicured gardens, limiting their growth to maintain an appearance of control. This rules out uncertainty but also growth. What has made us so willing to exchange risk for complacency, potential for mediocrity?

Often we ignore inklings of passion because we are focused on pleasing others—customers, coworkers, friends, family—rather than ourselves. How often have I heard people say they need to be a tougher boss, a more patient parent, or a more conscientious employee. Rarely do they say, "I need to be a better me."

In the same vein, we often make decisions based on what we think others will condone. We take a job because it pays well or the title sounds important, not because it is really what we want or are excited about. It is, after all, hard to ignore the ads for luxury automobiles and Caribbean cruises. Even the most directionless of twentysomething television characters has a pricey co-op in Manhattan furnished in velvets and hardwoods. Admit it. We feel compelled to work to have the same types of things, not because we care about them (although we may) but because we are trained to think we need them. Only when we have them do we consider ourselves successful.

What could take us farther from our heart? Made in succession, month after month, year after year, these types of decisions lead us farther and farther away from our passions, and ultimately from our happiness. Don't get me wrong; money is important. But selling your soul or betraying your heart is not the best way to gain it. What, after all, are possessions worth if they are financed at the expense of happiness?

BRINGING PASSION BACK

To be the best that we can, to be thrilled with our lives, we need to become self-fulfilling. We need to start from the heart. To do this, we must break down the barriers that prevent passion from flowing into our lives. We must rely on ourselves and on our passion to turn our hopes into reality. We need to make decisions based on the desires of our heart and not on the prescriptions of the world. When we do so, we open the floodgates to unimagined energy, commitment, and inspiration that—when accompanied by careful consideration— moves us far closer to our goals than any misguided reliance on common fallacy.

To begin to rediscover passion, you must understand your personal demons—the emotions that prevent you from pursuing passion freely. They must be acknowledged before they can be conquered.

Deterrents to Passion

There are many of these, and even passioneers know them well. You may recognize some of them in yourself:

Fear—There is no greater impediment to personal progress. Our greatest fear is the unknown. Passion is a mystery; often we do not know where it will lead us or what it might make us. You may wonder what life would be like if you followed your heart and changed careers or took on new challenges. Happier or more successful, you might imagine for a moment—and then fear steps in and you create elaborate scenarios of failure. If I was considering taking up ballroom dancing for fun, which should be relatively risk-free, under the influence of fear I might wonder, "What if the instructor is weird? What if I break my ankle? What if I can't find a parking spot? What if my partner has two left feet?"—any excuse to prevent the slightest discomfort that change might bring. And almost certainly I would wonder, "What if I make an absolute fool of myself? What will everyone think of me?"

Self-doubt—This is an extension of fear that focuses strictly on our personal inadequacies. It makes us question our abilities and our potential. Let's assume you have a passion for learning and are considering applying for graduate school. If you are battling self-doubt, you might stare at the application for weeks before finally tossing it out, thus nipping your passion in the bud. Self-doubt leads us to imagine ourselves becoming a failure rather than a success, miserable rather than happy. Succumb to it and you are powerless to embrace your passion.

Paralysis—When confused or uncertain, we have a tendency to freeze up and prevent ourselves from making a change. Paralysis of the heart afflicts us at times when we need our passion most—when we need the boost of adrenaline and self-confidence it can inspire. I have a colleague who was deeply unhappy in his job and longed to find a new one, but for some reason he could not bring himself to look. He knew he wanted and needed it, but nothing in his life inspired or empowered him to take the step. Whatever passion he possessed was trapped in the grip of emotional paralysis.

Numbness—Some become so accustomed to the demands and stresses of life that they move beyond paralysis into numbness. They no longer know what brings them pleasure or pain; all experiences simply blur together in a continuum of emotional disconnectedness. Someone who is numb might be miserable at work, but be unable to identify his job as the source of his unhappiness. Perhaps he has felt apathetic for so long that he assumes it is the way things are supposed to be. He is not acutely aware that he is unhappy, but he is also not aware that he is missing the joy that accompanies passion.

Limited Scope—In this age of special interests, we tend to define ourselves by category: male or female, black or white or brown, white collar or blue collar, twentysomething or Baby Boomer. This may help us identify with others in similar circumstances, but it limits the scope of what we come to expect or hope for. When we label ourselves in this fashion, we accept a gamut of characterizations that have nothing to do with who we really are or what is in our heart. For instance, because my sister is a woman she shares certain traits and experiences with other women. This does not mean, however, that she should only do things that other women have done. Nor should she alter her expectations to fit those of other women. She is first and foremost an individual, and thereby subject to the desires and longings of her own heart. Her heart knows no gender or ethnicity unless she so instructs it.

Being a member of a minority group, I have faced these issues many times. Not long ago I was asked by an Asian business organization to deliver a keynote address at one of its annual events. I was honored, looked forward to sharing some lessons I have learned as an entrepreneur over the years, and was considering the invite. But as the date approached I realized I had forgotten to ask what they wanted me to speak about. "Succeeding as an Asian-American," I was told. My response was immediate and decisive: I apologized but said I could not speak on that topic. It was antithetical to everything

I believe has been responsible for my success. I had succeeded as a human being, not as a member of an ethnic minority. I had never viewed my race as a hindrance or an aid in building my career or my life.

Procrastination—Laziness and procrastination prevent many people from making the changes they know passion can bring. How many times have you heard someone say, "I'm going to quit my job as soon as I have enough money saved" or "I'm going to pick up that hobby again as soon as I have more time." Not surprisingly they never find enough money or time to make a change. What they really lack, though, is initiative. Making excuses makes it impossible for passion to emerge.

Caution—Even those who do make moves often do so in ways so controlled and calculated that they leave little if any room for passion to enter it. They might not want to test the waters of the unknown or push the limits of their abilities to discover or develop their passions. The overly cautious may never know failure but they will also never know the success that comes with unleashing their passion.

I am no stranger to these deterrents. I strive daily to keep them out of my life. Most of the time, when things are going well, I cannot imagine entertaining them. But then there are times when, for one reason or another, I have a momentary lapse and let just a smidgen of doubt or fear run through my body. As long as my passion is alive and thriving, I can put on a brave face and work my way through these challenges. I remember a time when I nearly let self-doubt change the course of my life.

I was a graduate student studying psychology and was eager to begin helping others (one of my many passions) through an internship. I went one afternoon to be interviewed by an adviser for just such a position. After about fifteen minutes this man, who I now realize was incredibly callous and not the least bit insightful, rendered a verdict that was unsolicited and unwarranted. He told me, "Richard, you don't have what it takes to make it in this field." There it was. With those few words he dismissed countless hours of study, thought, and preparation. I was stunned. I responded with anger, but it later turned to self-doubt. The next few days were very difficult. I began to question my ability and also the validity of my passion. I knew I wanted to help people, but maybe my desire was not strong enough. How could I not be good enough?

As time passed, my passion came to the rescue. No matter how much my head tried to convince me that what the adviser had said was true, my heart would not stand for it. He had offended my passion, and it was not to be subdued. It was authentic and strong. With a burning in my soul, I sorted through what he had said and realized it was one man's opinion and nothing more. I could still help people. More importantly, I still wanted to. So I would.

Passion Review

Deterrents to Passion

- Fear
- Self-doubt
- Paralysis
- Numbness
- Limited Scope
- Procrastination
- Caution

I came within a hair of abandoning my passion, at least temporarily, because of the self-doubt this man planted in me. If I had I would have felt like so many people do today—trapped. In moments of weakness we succumb to negativity and begin to view ourselves as victims—of circumstance, of fate, of life. Though we cannot see it when it happens, we enslave ourselves. We don the shackles; we create our own cages.

DON'T ASK WHY, ASK WHY NOT

In reality we are not trapped unless we choose to be. If when confronted with challenges or tests of mettle we back down and deny our self-knowledge, we make it easy for all the forces that sap and kill passion to enter. Instead of asking ourselves why (Why should I take a risk? Why would I be any better than anyone else? Why should I try?), we need to ask why not. With your passion in play you will be supercharged, super-able. You will take risks because it is the only way to reap rewards. You will be better because you care. You will try because if you don't you will always regret it.

If passion is not part of your life now, do not think I am trivializing your situation. I understand the feelings of helplessness that may accompany it; I have been there. But I also understand the power of passion even for the most confused and skeptical of souls. I have seen it transform people, some gradually, some overnight. No matter how trapped you feel now, passion can get you out. It can change your life.

When you let passion in, the barriers to happiness and excellence seem smaller and you feel more motivated and empowered to break them down. You will be excited; you will have the energy to accomplish more and the courage to doubt yourself less. You will make choices that build up your spirit rather than tear it down. You will be uplifted and invigorated.

Begin Today

If you agree that passion is wanting in your life and desire to begin to bring it back, you must first commit to start from the heart. As you consider your life—where you are now and where you want to go—give priority to the promptings of your heart. You must trust it. Do not disparage or discredit your feelings. Accept them and then move forward with them. This does not mean you will follow them blindly or ignorantly, simply that you give credence to them and realize that they are an integral part of you.

Once you acknowledge your passions, you can then begin to shape them and follow them to whatever ends you seek. As you integrate them into the fabric of your existence, the life you lead will evolve from a life into your life. It will become an accurate reflection of your hopes and desires, your sensitivities and sensibilities. Most important, you will self-actualize. You will become the person you want to be, the person you know you can be.

Before you move on to Step Two, recall what you must do to fulfill Step One—to start from the heart. Remember each of the following points.

To help you begin to take these steps, complete Worksheet #1, which is the first step in your personal Passion Plan. List your high-priority passion sources in Section A, or those situations and experiences that have repeatedly elicited

Passion Review

To start from the heart I will . . .
- Commit to following my heart
- Break down the barriers to passion in my life
- Decide to become the person I really want to be

passion-related emotions. This will begin the process of identifying your passions, which you will further refine in Step Two. Then brainstorm the forces that might be preventing passion from working in your life in Section B, followed by potential ways you might seek to overcome them. This will give you a better idea of what you must move out of your life in order to move passion in.

Once you complete the worksheet and feel you are prepared to begin listening to your heart, move on to the next chapter to discover your passions.

PASSION PLAN WORKSHEET #1

Step 1: Start from the Heart	How
A. "High-Priority" Passion Sources:	List personal examples that accurately and clearly describe specific situations and/or times in your life when you were . . . • thrilled to be alive • exuberant • enthralled • exhilarated • experiencing rushes of enthusiasm Note: situations and experiences that repeatedly elicit feelings like those listed above are typically "higher priority" sources of passion.
B. Primary Passion Deterrent(s): *Deterrent* *Ways to Overcome*	Which deterrents, if any, have prevented you from building passion in your life? What can you do to overcome the deterrent? Deterrents may include but not be limited to . . . • Fear • Self-doubt • Paralysis • Numbness • Limited scope • Procrastination • Caution

CHAPTER 4

Step Two
Discover Your Passions

Know thyself.
THE SEVEN SAGES

Now that you have a window into the world of passion, it is time to get in touch with your own. If I were to ask you now what your passions are, could you name them? If you were like many people I talk to, you would answer, "I'm not sure. I'll have to get back to you on that one." So many of us are so busy juggling responsibilities that we have become strangers to our passion. We may get small glimpses, little moments of enjoyment and inspiration, but rarely do we benefit from continual or prolonged periods of passion. Our life simply does not reflect our heart.

WHAT DO YOU WANT TO BE WHEN YOU GROW UP?

A friend of mine recently was having a discussion with her three-year-old about action figures and preschool friends, when suddenly the topic changed. He asked, "Mommy, what do you want to be when you grow up?" She had not considered this question in many years, but it was every bit as relevant now as when she was a child. She is a successful attorney but realized saying so would not be an honest answer to the toddler's question. She could not put her finger on it, but she knew she had not become what she truly wanted to be. She answered, "I don't know, sweetie. What do you want to be?"

"I want to be a policeman," he replied. "But you could be an astronaut. Abby wants to be an astronaut. You could be one with her." Touched, she realized that although it was a little late to join the space program, she could be many other things. Not just in a career, but in life. She found herself wondering what really excited her about life. If she could be anything, if there were no limitations or obstacles, what would she be? A simple question from her son inspired her to reflect more intently than any professional seminar or counseling session ever had.

Few people could answer this question any differently than my friend did. Even if proud of what we have accomplished, perhaps even if we enjoy what we do, we cannot say that we have truly become who we wanted to be. Given the opportunity we might make some changes; we know we can do more, be better, be happier. But we don't know how. To begin to build the life we want, we need to embrace our passions. And to do that, we must first discover them.

For most, this is no simple task. As Socrates asked his pupil Meno over two thousand years ago, "When I don't know what a thing is, how can I know its quality?" We are in a catch-22. We cannot experience the power of our passion if we do not know what inspires it, and we cannot determine what inspires it if we do not experience it. There is no easy way around this dilemma, but your heart does give you an advantage. Given the right conditions, it will speak to you. It will provide the clues to help you find where your passions lie.

WAYS TO DISCOVER PASSION

There are many times and many ways to get in touch with your passion. In this chapter I will show you how others have done so and I suggest how you can do the same. As you read, remember that you can bring passion back into your life and that you are entitled to it. You do not need to fear it or back down from it. You can live with intensity. You can become who you want to be.

Discovery by Epiphany: "I Knew When..."

From as early as she can remember, Karen's parents told her she was going to be a nurse. Her father was a doctor, her mother a nurse, so to them it seemed an obvious choice. Karen felt otherwise. She was not drawn to medicine and actually had a distaste for the tools of the trade—needles, syringes, gauges, and monitors. Always obedient, Karen agreed to attend nursing school but secretly planned to abandon the field once she graduated. She convinced herself the skills she learned would be useful regardless of the career she ended up choosing, and therefore her time would not be wasted.

Because Karen's heart was not in her studies, her performance in school was mediocre. As the semesters passed, she looked forward to telling her parents she was finished with nursing and moving on. She was not sure what she wanted to be, but she knew it was not a nurse, or anything related to medicine.

Then, suddenly, her thinking changed. Karen was volunteering at a local hospital to earn credit toward her degree. One night on her way out, she passed by the room of an elderly man. He was sitting on the edge of his bed, his head hanging in despair. He looked so pitiful, so frail; Karen knew she had to help. To this day, she does not know what overcame her. Usually a shy woman, something compelled her to enter his room and sit down beside him.

What she found shocked and appalled her. Two nurses were in the bathroom washing sheets, which apparently the old man had soiled. This is not uncommon, of course, but to Karen's surprise the nurses were griping loudly about it and callously disparaging the man as if he were not even in the room. Her throat tightened and tears welled in her eyes.

Calmly and quietly she took the man's hand and said, "Please don't listen to them. They have no right to talk to you this way. This is a job they are paid well to do. You just ignore them." She thought her words had had no effect because the man remained still and silent. Fearing she had made things worse, she got up to leave. But he grabbed her hand and, with tears in his eyes, spoke the two words that would change the course of Karen's life forever: "Thank you." At that moment she realized there was no other place she would rather be and nothing else she would rather be doing. She now understood that nursing was what she had to do. She had to help people, to take care of them. As a nurse she would be everything that the two women in that man's bathroom were not. She would be kind, caring, and respectful. That night it became clear to Karen that nursing is not about medications and measurements; it is about people.

She has been a nurse for over twenty years now and received many awards for her work. She finds this amusing because she has never played the game, so to speak. Many times she has taken years off and worked odd schedules to care for her four children, who, she emphasizes, are her first priority. From that day in the hospital, she has viewed her work as a privilege, not a duty. She is always eager to work and willing to learn. This has resulted in promotions she did not seek and opportunities she never imagined. Karen is still amazed that some people in her profession begrudge those they are paid to serve. To be a nurse and not love people simply makes no sense.

Karen's passion is helping others and nursing provides an ideal means of making that passion an integral part of her life. We could argue that she also has a passion for nursing itself. She admits that no other profession could provide her with the same opportunity to care for her fellow man in quite the same way. She also confesses that if she did not need the money she would still nurse. She loves it that much.

Karen's was a discovery of passion by epiphany: one pivotal, life-changing experience made her suddenly and intensely aware of it. The experience was unexpected; she did not seek it. It was powerful; in that single, clear moment the mystery surrounding her heart was revealed and she was left with a distinct impression of who she had to be. On that night her heart did not whisper, it yelled.

Many of us never have a moment like that. I have news, though: whatever your age, your epiphany may yet come. Epiphanies do not result from planning or deliberation. You cannot anticipate or formulate them. They can happen anywhere, anytime. Those who support chaos theory will argue they are the product of chance, of the randomness and unpredictability of life. Students of Plato and devotees of many religions will maintain that they are the workings of fate, events that are preordained by a heavenly force. Followers of Jung and new age theories will contend they are the result of synchronicity, that they are meaningful coincidences conspiring to teach you about your nature and purpose in life.

Whether you choose to read a deeper spiritual meaning into this type of personal revelation is your choice and no doubt a product of your belief system. Regardless of how you interpret epiphanies, though, my message to you is the same: you must embrace them. Whatever their cause, you must view them as valuable insights into the longings of your heart. You must not dismiss them as freakish or irrelevant, but as authentic and instructive. Above all, be grateful for the self-knowledge they inspire and use them to begin building a fulfilling life.

Discovery Through Change: "I Figured It Out After..."

The truth revealed by epiphany is instantaneous. Processing our reactions to it is peripheral; only later might we evaluate, explain, and analyze it.

But with discovery through change, such analysis is central. Major life changes such as birth or death, marriage or divorce, losing an old job or taking a new one, illness or recovery can alter our view of life and cause us to examine the way we live it. As we react, we may learn things about ourselves we never knew. This includes discovering our passions.

On a recent flight, I sat next to a prominent public figure; call him Ben. He shared with me how just such a change had enabled him to discover his passion. Ben had risen from a youth of urban poverty to become a respected politician. Surprisingly, it was not politics that saved him from the ghetto, but athletics. He was discovered in high school by a recruiter who was certain Ben's skill on the football field could land him first in a private school and possibly later at a prominent university. Ben accepted the scholarship he offered, and then, through a combination of academic and athletic performance, found his way into the Ivy League.

Ben might have left college a four-year letterman headed to a career in investment banking or coaching, but for one pivotal event. During a scrimmage, he broke his ankle. It would take months to heal, and he now was faced with more free time than he had ever known. Given his dynamic personality and active lifestyle, he knew he could not be idle during his recovery. At the suggestion of a friend, he decided to run for student office. Though he had not been active in student government before, he thought it might be a good outlet for his energies. Little did he know that it would become much, much more.

Preparing his campaign, Ben's passion broke free. He was filled with such excitement and energy that it was no surprise he won his office easily. He found politics moved him beyond anything he had ever experienced. He *knew* it was what he had to do in life. After graduation, Ben returned to his home state where he has since been elected to a number of public offices.

Though Ben was a talented athlete, athletics were not his passion. They served as a vehicle for him to discover what was. The major change brought about by his injury forced him to turn in new directions and explore new opportunities. One of those opportunities just happened to be something his heart was yearning for but had never known.

Ben's story does not involve tragedy, but others in this

category do. The women and children who founded Mothers Against Driving Drunk (MADD) and SADD, its student counterpart, might never have been prompted to feel or express their passion for social change if they had not lost sons, daughters, and friends. Christopher Reeve, the former Superman of the silver screen, might never have discovered his passion for motivating and inspiring others to challenge their limitations if he had not suffered his own personal tragedy when he was rendered quadriplegic after a horseback riding accident.

Nor does Ben's story involve the overwhelming joy that accompanies major life events such as marriage and birth. Parenthood is one of the most common and powerful causes of discovery through change. Our children provide us with a window into ourselves. We recognize ourselves in them and ponder what we will teach them, what of our nature and our experience we can share with them. In striving to build better lives for them, we are forced to reflect on our own hopes and dreams. They often inspire us to change our focus or our outlook. The responsibility of caring for them can render changes in our nature we never thought possible. A selfish woman can become a selfless mother. A lazy man can become a motivated father. Through these changes, we can experience emotions we have never felt and discover passions we have never identified.

Great works the world over might never have come to pass if the people who wrought them had not been affected by monumental change, if they had not had their passion ignited by a significant shift in life. For such people, passion becomes an outgrowth of their experience, a reaction to it.

If you have encountered such a change in your life and suppressed your reaction or denied its relevance, reexamine your feelings and look for the hints of passion they might reveal. If you experience such a change in the future, be prepared to look at it as instructive rather than destructive, to look for the positive instead of the negative, the enabling rather than the disabling.

Discovery Through Intuition: "I've Always Known..."

Discovering your passion is necessarily a product of intuition. You must sense your passion in order to identify it. All of us have intuition; fewer recognize the cues it sends. Some seem to be born with such strong intuition that from a very early age—sometimes even infancy—they sense and understand their passions. The power of their intuition is expressed as certainty: they know their passion and are confident in it. With fearlessness and conviction they embrace it fully and follow the course it dictates.

These people we categorize as dreamers, people who pursue their passions in wealth or in poverty, in good times or bad. Often they are artists, actors, writers, or musicians—people compelled by their passion to create. They are also entrepreneurs and heads of state—people compelled by their passion to lead. And they are nuns and advocates of the downtrodden—people compelled by their passion to serve. Something about their nature allows their passion to flow unabated. Once it is unleashed it is so powerful that they cannot ignore it, they must follow it. This is true whether their environments feed their passions or stifle them. A child who must draw in the absence of crayons will use mud or toothpaste or lipstick. A child who must write in the absence of pen and paper will spin stories in her head or share them with friends. The passion of these people will not be confined. It finds ways to express itself and work its way into their lives.

We recognize this when we say "He's a born leader" or "She's a natural." We may both revere and fear people for it. We desire what they have but doubt that we can feel as strongly as they do.

So many figures in world history—both famous and infamous—fall into this category that I could fill the pages of this book just listing them. It is, I contend, the power of their passion that propels them to prominence. Many others do not gain fame but still sense their passion early and follow it throughout their days. Jesse is one.

Jesse is a creator—of stories, of ideas, of worlds. Currently she designs computer games for large software companies. She spends her days spinning fables of overlords and underworlds, heroes and villains, fantasy and science fiction. In no uncertain terms, she says, "I love what I do." But her creativity does not end with work: it flows into her home, into her leisure, and remains with her through the ups and downs, ins and outs of her life. It is, in a nutshell, who she is.

Jesse's own description of the role passion has played and continues to play in her life is will worth including in its entirety here:

> I have always known I wanted to be a writer. At least, I was
> always interested in creating. I can remember being a little
> girl, and making up one song, over and over in the backseat
> of my mom's red Datsun, memorizing it so that when I was
> older I would have one song that somebody else hadn't
> thought up—I guess that week I thought I was going to be
> Helen Reddy. And I used to make books of characters—girls

in ball gowns, Martian ladies in space hats, and secretaries in work clothes, or what I thought were work clothes. They were all very glamorous with feathers and these forties-style high heels. I invented books of fairy tales, all about the never-ending travails of Princess Primrose. And I played endless imagination games with my little brother, dressing him up in ballerina tutus, making him be my genie, the student in my class, the baby to my mother.

But most of all I remember reading. I was shy and I would steal up into the tree in our backyard with a pillow and read for hours. I remember my mother reading to me in the car, and crying in Barstow when we were crossing the Mojave Desert because of something that happened to the boy in *The Red Badge of Courage*. I don't remember what now. I sat on the floor of my closet and waited to be transported into Narnia. I suppose I knew I wouldn't really be taken there—but I guess I felt there was some honor in acting out the desire.

When I entered grade school, I became very bored. By the first grade, I was having real problems. One day, I climbed out of the window and walked the six blocks to my house. I shut myself in my room and started writing reports on countries from the *World Book Children's Encyclopedia*. Making up countries, real and pretend. Soon after, I was tested for learning difficulties and sent to a gifted school. At that school, we could schedule our time as we pleased. I scheduled reading, all day, every day. The pattern continued. I went to a college where there were no requirements and I took thirty-six English classes—literature and writing. I also wrote plays and dabbled in the humanities. By graduate school, I was teaching and writing, but also working as a writer in Hollywood.

Now I create universes and write for video and computer
games—so you see, mine is literally the case of someone who
discovered her passion when she was five or six years old
and stayed with it her entire life.

I can't imagine not writing. For me, reading and writing—the
process of taking things out of life and putting things back in—
has come to fundamentally affect my psyche, my family, my
sense of myself and the meaning of my life. When I am writing
a character, I am writing the perspective of that character, or
becoming that individual for a time. That empathic process is
how I understand life, understand people. I can't really explain
it much beyond this: when I am writing people, I am using a
compassionate ability to feel what they are feeling. In a strange
way, I love the people I am writing about, and I love myself
when I am writing about them. It's some feeling of connection
on a cosmic scale. I love life when I am writing. When I am not
regularly writing, I feel disconnected, out of touch, out of love.
But when I write, I love things and people, and myself.

What Jesse expresses so eloquently is the power of passion
to transform and guide our lives. Like so many other passioneers, she considers herself lucky to be living the life she is
living. She is lucky, not because someone did something for her
or something happened to her but because she recognized her
guiding passion at such a young age. Everything she has
accomplished is the result of commitment to that passion, and
her life is fulfilling because of it.

Discovery Through Experience: "I'm Not Sure How I Figured It Out..."

Most of us fall into the fourth and final category of discovery:
discovery through experience. We discover our passions not

instantaneously as lightning bolts of inspiration, not forceful-ly as reactions to major events, not mysteriously as the truth of our existence. We uncover them gradually as a result of day-to-day experience. We get glimpses of them courtesy of intu-ition, but we do not understand their significance nor heed their influence.

The problem is that this usually has little or no impact. The messages are there, and they may be from our heart, but they are subtle. Unless we pick up on them and pay atten-tion—and many of us cannot—we are likely to dispel them. They are neither earth shattering nor life changing. The chal-lenge becomes to learn to interpret the signals our heart sends and translate them into action, into pursuit.

A young executive I know, let's call him Zack, recently made such a discovery after years of denying what was in his heart. When Zack was a child he had many interests. He was a gifted athlete, a talented student, and a creative spirit. He entertained notions of playing professional football (as his father had done), studying to be a doctor, and becoming a uni-versity president. Given the range of his abilities and the level of his determination, his parents were sure any of these were well within his reach. As Zack worked his way through high school and then college, he gradually whittled away at his options. Though he was fascinated by the biology of the human body, he was not eager to devote long study to it. Though recruited by many football powerhouses, he elected to attend an Ivy League college and give priority to developing his intellect rather than his physical prowess. He held on to his dream of leading a university, but realized he would need to distinguish himself in some area in preparation for such an office.

In college, Zack discovered that he had a knack for many things he had never considered. He had a gift for speaking foreign languages and a talent for programming computers. Mathematics came naturally to him, and as director of the intramural program for his dormitory he discovered an underlying proclivity for leadership. But writing stories was a skill that most surprised him and appeared on the surface not to suit him. Zack had always enjoyed making up stories but, suffering from a form of dyslexia commonly known as bad speller's syndrome, he had never considered writing them down. The frustration was simply too great.

Zack's mother was always active in his education and repeatedly asked his teachers to work with him on writing. She remembers with frustration the comment of his fourth-grade teacher: "It doesn't matter if he can write well, Mrs. Jenkins; he'll have a secretary to help him." This infuriated her; she did not want her son to be deficient in any area, and she certainly did not appreciate the teacher's assumptions. But Zack had expressed no interest in writing-intensive professions, so she hoped it would never become an issue.

Zack's high school teachers were no better. They were in awe of his intelligence and figured that weak writing would not interfere with his success. But in college, good writing was critical. Zack struggled to overcome his limitations with modest success. After gaining some confidence, he applied for a spot in a creative writing seminar. He submitted a short story he had written over the previous summer and then waited. When the list of students accepted for the course was posted, his name was not on it. He was crushed, but not about to give up. He petitioned the instructor and wrangled his way into the class.

From the first meeting he felt out of place. The stories he

wrote were humorous and strange—but they were stories. The other students proffered material that was highly symbolic but devoid of the characteristics that traditionally define a story. From their self-appointed role as representatives of literary art, they made him feel guilty about his love of storytelling and inadequate as a writer. His first creative writing class also became his last.

After graduation, Zack landed a fantastic job with a small start-up software company. He got his feet wet in product design, sales, marketing, and management. In a matter of years, he became director at a large software company and seemed poised for a long and illustrious career in the world of technology. But something was wrong. He knew it. He was not happy. Living in New York, he was surrounded by people working in creative roles—designers, artists, directors, and writers. In the company of such people, his urge to create, to write stories resurfaced.

He began by jotting down his ideas and within months had written a collection of short stories. He found that even if writing served no other purpose it made him happy. It gave an outlet to his passion and helped him realize who he was. Though Zack and Jesse, the writer I mentioned earlier, share a love of writing, Zack did not experience the force of his passion as a child. In fact, everything about his childhood discouraged him from finding it—his talent in other areas, his weakness in the mechanics of writing, the ignorance of his teachers. Though he has lived with great zest and always been a go-getter, his life never felt complete until he discovered writing, his passion.

Today Zack is still working in software, but he has plans to move into publishing once he has refined his writing skills and found his voice. Though he would like to succeed in the

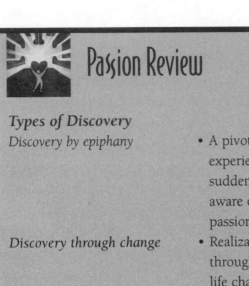

Passion Review

Types of Discovery

Discovery by epiphany	• A pivotal, life changing experience that makes you suddenly and intensely aware of an underlying passion
Discovery through change	• Realization of a passion through reaction to a major life change such as birth, marriage, divorce, or death of a friend or loved one
Discovery through intuition	• An inborn and undeniable awareness of one's passion.
Discovery through experience	• Gradual awareness of passion through day-to-day experiences

eyes of the world, his happiness does not rely on it. By discovering his passion and allowing it to influence his decisions and his direction, he has created his own success.

STEPS TO DISCOVERY

If you have lost touch with your passions or never knew them, there is much you can do to find them. Depending on your circumstances, it will take varying effort. If you are no stranger to your passion, perhaps all you need to do is slow down and evaluate what about your life keeps you excited and feeds your energy. But if your life is devoid of passion, if you have been suppressing it for many years, discovery may entail many months of introspection and experimentation.

The steps to discovery fall into the same phases as the Passion Plan itself: feel, think, and act. First, take a step back from your life, literally and figuratively. In order to listen to your heart you must somehow shut out the day-to-day noise, stress, and confusion and seek perspective on your life. Doing this might require only a quiet walk in the woods or a night in front of the fire; however, if you feel you cannot escape so easily, you might need to retreat completely. This could mean flying halfway around the globe or loading a tent into the back of the car and spending a few days in the mountains.

Perspective is critical to your discovery because it eliminates the trivialities and perceptions that distract you from listening to your heart. Given distance, matters of seemingly great urgency become insignificant. Issues that predominate our thinking and absorb our energy seem inconsequential. And goals that seem critical to our success recede in prominence.

Commit to taking a step back from your life. You do not need to leave your city or even your home, but you must make it possible to examine your life without being consumed by it. This means no phone calls, faxes, e-mails, or printouts. No screaming children, no doting significant others, no meddlesome neighbors. No mailman, no TV repairman, no Girl Scouts selling cookies. It means peace, possibly silence, and definitely solitude. Others cannot help you at this stage—later, certainly, but not now.

Once you have found the time and place to reflect, sit down, breathe deeply, and try to relax. Then answer the following questions, but do not stop with the first thoughts that pop into your head. Pay attention to how you feel. Listen for the answers your heart provides.

Where am I today? Ponder your life as it is. Are you happy with the direction you are going? Do you have a direction, or are you just letting life lead you where it will? Do you want things to change? If so, how? Do you want a different job, a different environment, new friends? How do you feel about your life in general? Are you excited, hopeful, apathetic, depressed? Is the life you are leading a true reflection of who you are?

Where do I want to be tomorrow? If you could wake up tomorrow without the shortcomings and fears you have today, how would you be different? Where would you turn for happiness? How would you spend your time? What would you try to achieve?

What do I regret in my life? What actions in your life do you wish you could undo? Which choices would you make differently given the chance? What risks did you walk away from? What opportunities didn't you take?

I realize answering these questions is not easy. Summing up your life over the course of a few minutes, an hour, or even a day is a tremendous challenge. Even if you cannot respond in detail, however, you should have a rough sense of the task that lies before you. You should have an intuition of the distance between where you are now and where you want to be, and a feeling as to the scope of change that will be required to get there.

With this rather fuzzy awareness, you are ready to begin to identify your passions. They are, after all, the key to your progress. They will provide the incentive to move you from the life you have to the life you want and improve the quality of your experience as you get there.

Look to the Past

To begin, remember your childhood and the intensity with which you lived it. Think about the things you loved to do and the way you felt while doing them. When your parents couldn't find you, what did they assume you were doing? Did you disappear into nature—parks, forests, beaches—to explore? Did you spend hours on end in your room assembling model airplanes or building racecourses for your toy cars? Did you sing, dance, or hammer away at the piano? Did you mediate disputes between your friends, lead them into imaginary battles, or organize their neighborhood productions? What caught your interest and held it (no small achievement for a child)? What did you dream of doing? What did you brag to friends you were going to do or be when you grew up? Were your boasts grounded in true desire or meant to impress? What subjects did you enjoy in school? Why?

After you've considered all these questions and sifted through your memories, make a list of all these passion candidates from the past. As you look over the list, what emotions come over you? Can you remember the feelings these things inspired? Do you think you are capable of feeling them again?

Perhaps some of the items on your list are still in your life today. If so, they likely are passions for you. Those that are not could have been diversions of youth, passing amusements, or potential passions you have since repressed. Consider why each activity you no longer engage in fell out of your life. Did you make the choice yourself out of lack of interest, or did you let someone else make the decision for you? Did your parents tell you the interest was impractical, too dangerous, or not respectable? Were you afraid you did not have the talent or ability to keep pursuing it into adulthood? Did you do it less and less over the years until eventually you forgot about it completely? If you stopped doing something for reasons other than your own, you may well have abandoned passion along the way.

This was true for a friend of mine who as a child dreamed of being a professional dancer. At her begging, her mother signed her up for dance classes when she was ten. She proved quite talented and what little she lacked in natural ability she compensated for with spirit. She was truly passionate about dance both as discipline and art, and her performances sparkled. As the years passed she grew in ability but her confidence waned. Though she was thin as a rail, her instructors told her she was too short to make it in a top ballet company. Faced with an obstacle only genetics could overcome, she had begun to doubt her potential. Her fear was compounded by the fact that her peers, most of whom had begun dancing at the age of five or six, did their best to make her feel inferior for the years of training she had missed.

Then, the summer before her fifteenth birthday, she visited her grandmother, who after teaching high school for more than thirty years considered herself an expert on teenagers. Learning of her granddaughter's plans for a dancing career, she scoffed, "You'll quit. Mark my words. You think that's what you want now, but you'll give it up sooner or later. I've seen it happen over and over." My friend was crushed. Her grandmother had not intended to level a personal attack, but nonetheless her words cut like a knife.

Though my friend continued her lessons for another year, she never recovered from that final blow. She became ashamed of her dream. When the time came to begin auditioning for professional companies, she backed down, emotionally defeated. As an adult the pain of her decision has lessened, but the regret remains. She will never know if she could have made it as a professional dancer: time has robbed her of that privilege. But her passion lingers. In examining her life recently she realized that despite the years that have passed she still loves dancing. Even if not as a professional dancer, she can find ways to work the passion, and the excitement and fulfillment it brings, back into her life.

Look to the Present

You have already taken a look at your life in the general sense; now consider the details. What about your life right now do you love, or at least enjoy? What do you actively dislike, and what do you merely tolerate? Which activities do you undertake eagerly and which do you only endure? What is your favorite aspect of your job, and why? What do you look forward to from day to day? What would you miss most if it was taken away?

After making a preliminary list, look for connections between the items on it. Perhaps the things you enjoy most share a common theme: helping, learning, leading. Maybe they center on a particular topic: architecture, animals, the stock market. Perhaps they require you to push yourself to the limit or maybe they allow you to retreat into the comfort of your abilities.

Think also of the conditions most conducive to your feeling excitement or happiness. Where do you feel most vital? What about those settings do you enjoy? The people, the physical space, the activity that goes on there? Which people in your life make you feel the most alive? What about them do you admire most? What traits or qualities do you share? Which times of day do you have the most energy? What are you doing during these times?

The answers should help you develop a picture of your life in your mind's eye. You should be able to see patterns to your happiness and perhaps even determine the specific causes. The passions that are present in your life now might have already been obvious to you, but you might be surprised: some sources of inspiration you may never have identified. This is true because passion can work in subtle as well as monumental ways. Traces of surface emotion may reveal feelings that run much deeper. As the English explorer and writer Sir Walter Raleigh explained to Elizabeth I, "Our passions are most like to floods and streams, The shallow murmur, but the deep are dumb." Dumb meaning silent here, of course. Our deepest passions do not necessarily make themselves known. They sometimes work within us quietly, manifesting in small moments and small ways.

When an acquaintance approached me about helping her discover her passions, I asked her to take the very steps proposed here. Though she felt her life moving in a positive direction, she described herself as lacking in enthusiasm and intensity: she was suffering from passion deficit. This surprised me because she had a career that by definition seemed exciting. She was a fashion model who, though not famous, was recognized and respected locally. But she felt a certain emptiness about modeling. She enjoyed the shows and shoots but wasn't sure why. She liked the extravagant clothes and the loud music, but always felt a little uncomfortable with the attention they brought her.

I asked her to note her specific reactions during her next show. When we met again, she was almost embarrassed. "It's the makeup," she said, and, when I seemed confused, she explained that the time she enjoyed most was prior to the show when the makeup artists transform the girls-next-door into icons of glamour. Something about the metamorphosis intrigued and excited her. At my suggestion, she has found ways to incorporate this fascination into her life beyond the occasional fashion event. She now claims the faces of family and friends as her canvases and works her own version of cosmetic artistry on any who are willing to submit. She takes notes from the artists at her shows and is rapidly building up her own arsenal of lip liners, eye shadows, and blush brushes. Where she will go with this newly realized curiosity is unclear. She is still experimenting, still learning about herself and her interest. But she has made a start and has very possibly discovered a passion.

Look to the Future

Earlier I asked you to consider where you want to be tomorrow, what kind of changes you might want to make in your life today. Now think about the future in a greater, more idealistic sense. What things do you hope for most? If all obstacles and limitations were removed, what would you want to do, accomplish, be? Hidden within your dreams, your grandest fantasies, are clues to your passions. Do not worry if they seem unrealistic, perhaps even unattainable; they still reflect passions that can be realized in more down-to-earth ways. If, for example, you long to live on a remote tropical island, perhaps you have an unrealized passion, and need, for solitude or sunshine. A vision of being famous may reveal a desire, perhaps even a passion, for acceptance and acknowledgment. Even if you are an accountant and your dream is to be a jockey, there may be meaning to it. Maybe you have a fondness for horses, a passion for riding, a competitive spirit, or a secret desire to be showered in flowers.

Even if the connection between fantasy and reality is not immediately obvious, take this valuable step toward uncovering your passions. Make a list of the things you dream for and take time to think about what they might mean to you now. What do they tell you about yourself? How might they pertain in your life today?

I asked a colleague to describe his vision of his future. In twenty years, he said, he imagined himself rising to the upper echelons of his current company, or one similar to it, and taking two vacations per year instead of one. Disappointed, I prodded further: "If you could be doing anything in twenty years, what would it be?" The response was far more encouraging: "I think I would want to head a humanitarian organization and serve on the board of a few big companies." But it amazed me that even though both of these things were within the bounds of reality, he viewed them as far fetched. Achieving them would require work, namely wise management of his career options and some political savvy, but he stood a decent chance of bringing them about.

Musing further, he acknowledged a strong desire to be involved in shaping the future. As he explained, he grew more animated. After a few minutes he was talking so fast I could

barely understand him. It became obvious that he is a vision-
ary, someone with big ideas for improving institutions and the
roles they play in society. He was brimming with ideas and
hopes but didn't think he was qualified or poised to offer them
to the world. I pointed out that his enthusiasm and knowledge
were convincing and that regardless of whether he decided to
act on his dreams, he should find ways to develop and share
his ideas with others. They obviously meant a great deal to
him and were worthy candidates for his time and attention.

Step Back In

Once you return from your step back, whether it took you to
another country or just another room, take action to uncover
your passion as you go about your normal routine. First, look
around your home, your office, any place you spend time, and
notice the types of things you surround yourself with. What
kind of books do you read? What kind of movies do you see?
What kind of people do you like to be around? Your heart
reveals itself through such clues. If you love to read about science, then maybe something about science is a passion for
you—discovery, analysis, or inquiry; planets, atoms, or under-
sea life. If you hang out with artists even though you are not
one yourself, perhaps you have a creative passion you see mir-
rored in them.

Now, as you begin to evaluate your life from close prox-
imity, you can turn to those who know you well for added
insight. Schedule some time with your confidants—friends,
spouse, boss, children, parents—to discuss you, and just you.
Ask them to name your strengths and weaknesses, your talents
and abilities as they see them. Do this not because they know

you better than you know yourself but because they see your passion from another perspective. You might get so caught up in what you are doing that you fail to make your own judgments. Think about it. Has anyone ever surprised you with a statement like "You were great" or "That was amazing"? Perhaps it was after you made a presentation, dribbled a ball down the court, or juggled five tasks simultaneously. Whatever the case, the comment caught you off guard because you were so focused on doing what you were doing that you did not realize you were doing it so well. This is a telltale sign of passion-heightened performance—and it is entirely possible that you are unaware of your passion as you engage in activities that inspire it.

You might be surprised to learn that often we are equally oblivious to the moods we project to others. I remember a woman in college who always had something unfavorable to say about the food in the campus dining hall. Often it was couched in humor, but the impression it left was anything but humorous. She came off as a complainer, even a whiner. When someone finally asked her why she continued to dine in the facility, she was shocked. She said she actually enjoyed the food and never realized that she was being so negative. After pondering her behavior, she realized it was her underlying attitude toward food—she would rather hook up to an IV than eat three times a day—that was expressing itself. What had been hidden from her own view was readily apparent to others. In a sense, they had grown to know her better than she knew herself.

The same can be true of our passions. You might have recognized this in someone close to you. Have you ever found yourself thinking, "He's so much happier when he's working with his hands" or "Her face lights up whenever we talk about traveling." Sometimes, others can detect signals from our heart even before we can. If we feel guilty for enjoying a particular activity, we may convince ourselves we don't really like it. Likewise, if we feel pressured to appreciate something we really dislike, we might persuade ourselves it is as wonderful as everyone else says it is. No matter how well we have been conditioned to conceal our true emotions, they do reveal themselves to others. Use this to your advantage. Let your friends and family help you gain a window back into your passion.

I did, not so long ago. In my job, I spend a lot of time teaching and counseling clients. I have always enjoyed addressing large groups and pride myself in the public speaking skills I have developed over the years. Meeting with coworkers one afternoon, one suggested that my speaking skills are strong, but my ability to engage an audience in question and answer sessions is more profound. She noted that when I pick up the microphone and move among the crowd I seem more animated and absorbed than when behind the podium. Reviewing a seminar videotape later, I realized she was right: during Q&A I moved differently, I spoke differently. At the next such meeting I was aware of this energy as it emerged. I was truly in a flow state, and the reason was the excitement I felt about the topic and about sharing it with the audience. Based on this newfound awareness, I began to think of ways I might integrate this passion more fully into my life. Among other things, it has led to my work on the creation of a television talk-show concept centered on workplace improvement issues. It has helped me expand my vision of the future and target new avenues for spreading my passion to others.

Begin to Experiment

If after reflecting, pondering, observing, and discussing you still cannot identify your passions, it is time to act. It is after all possible, though unlikely, that you have passed through the years of your life without touching on your passions in any significant way. If so, don the cloak of the passioneer and set out to explore the world. You need not seek out new lands, just new experiences, new people, and new activities. You must create opportunities for your passions to surface. Take a class at the local community college, apply for a part-time job, join a neighborhood athletic team, help a friend with his work, attend lectures and meetings, try a new hobby. Find out what your friends do for fun and join them. Experience the same old places and same old events through your kids' eyes. Look for the fresh in the stale, the old in the new.

If you are feeling really adventurous, you might be ready to take a bigger step. The most effective but also the most frightening move you can make is to force yourself out of your comfort zone and begin to take some risks. Though this might be painful at first, the discomfort you endure will one day seem a small price to pay for the self-awareness you gain. To take this step you will need to confront your fears head on. You will need to stare your weaknesses in the face and defy them. If you usually stand on the sidelines as an observer, jump in as a participant. If you feel intimidated by school, take a class. If you are hung up on process, start to focus on results. The point is not to do things you dislike, but to break down the barriers that might be preventing you from finding things you enjoy. Sometimes a change of this sort is just what you need to jolt yourself into a deeper awareness of who you are at heart.

When I think of pushing limits, I have to chuckle. In my life I have always felt an inexplicable need to put myself out on a limb, to test the limits of my abilities and my mettle. When I was ten my sister started roller skating, not just as an amusement but at a competitive level. I often watched her practice and put in a few laps around the rink here and there, but I never thought much about roller skating as a sport. My friends didn't do it. After all, it was dancing on wheels. One day when I accompanied my sister to the rink, a girl about my age asked me to skate during one of the infamous "couples skates." After we were through, she thought enough of my performance that she invited me to partner with her in competition. I'm not sure what possessed me, but I agreed.

Nothing had prepared me for that experience; competitive sports were not part of my world at the time. But when the girl asked me to partner, I dispelled my immediate doubts—would I embarrass myself, was it just for girls, would my friends laugh?—and took a risk, somehow knowing that if nothing else I would grow from the experience. We went on to become local and regional champions, but despite our success I knew roller skating was not a passion for me. It did, however, provide a way for my competitive passion to emerge, and I have actively pursued that passion ever since. Oddly enough it also showed me that I had a natural ability for choreographed movement, something I might never have learned otherwise. Dancing became something, like bowling, that I could do to play out my passion for competition. Over the years I have stomped, shuffled, hustled, and do-si-doed my way through contests, building my passion as well as my trophy collection.

Try Taste Tests

If you do not feel quite so daring, there are safer ways to experiment with passion. I call them taste tests. Once you have come up with a list of potential passions, you can begin to let them into your life on your own terms. If you remember how much you loved singing as a child, you might decide to take a few voice lessons before running out to join a choir. If you have always dreamed of writing a novel, jot down a storyline. If you are hoping to move into a new field, investigate schools and organizations that might help you learn more. If you think you might want to become a leader, volunteer with a children's group. Find ways to test your suspicions that are nonthreatening. Discovery will be more gradual than if you were to make more drastic changes, but you should begin to sense the things that move you.

These taste tests can also help you begin to distinguish where your passions lie with regard to certain activities. Perhaps one highlight of your week is coaching your daughter's soccer game. The next time you hit the field, try to figure out what about it really excites you. Is it leading and organizing the children? Instructing them? Devising plays and plans? Striving to win? The sport itself? Or is it simply spending time with your daughter? Once you have an idea, you can begin to test your instincts. If it's soccer you love, attend some professional games. Working with children? Volunteer at a school. Competition? Join a team yourself. Probably you enjoy many things about coaching, but by examining all the aspects you might learn what really lights your fire. You can then find other activities that allow you to express it.

Take Perspective Breaks

After you have had a chance to reflect (feel), counsel and examine (think), and experiment (act), you should begin to get a sense of your passion. As you engage in the process of discovery, continue to take perspective breaks. You do not need to retreat with the same intensity you did earlier, but you can do things that offer you varying views of your life. One is reading. It may not be a passion for you, but it is an invaluable source of inspiration and insight. Regardless of your interests, reading can expose you to new ideas and new frames of reference. Viewing the same old things through the eyes of another can cause you to see the world and your life in new ways, just as I hope this book is doing now.

Jesse described the empathy that takes over when she writes. Empathy is also the force that compels us to make self-discoveries when we read. You can probably remember reading *Moby Dick* or *Little Women* in school and seeing the world through the eyes of Ishmael or Jo. We share their experiences and through them have experiences of our own. Similarly, when we read the thoughts of great minds we make discoveries about our world that can actually challenge and change our perceptions of our role in it. As Thoreau said in 1854, "How many a man has dated a new era in his life from the reading of a book." Reading almost anything forces us to think and more important to feel. And any opportunity for feeling is an opportunity for passion to peek through.

Other activities also enable perspective-altering discovery. Traveling requires us to ponder what is meaningful at home and in the new places we see. Watching plays and

Passion Review

Steps to Discovery

Feel	*Think*	*Act*
• Relax	• Counsel	• Experiment
• Reflect	• Examine	• Try Taste Tests
• Listen	• Observe	• Take Perspective Breaks

movies, attending festivals and celebrations compels us to experience our own lives through the eyes of others and therefore see ourselves in new ways.

However earnest your efforts might be, your discovery will probably be gradual. If you have been suffering from passion deficit, it might take awhile to learn to discern between passion and interest. After you have identified your potential passion sources, you must pursue them. As you do, keep the following questions in mind when determining whether something is really a passion for you. The more yes answers you provide, the more likely it is you have discovered a passion.

Passion Litmus Test

1. Do you lose track of time when engaged in the activity?

2. Do you perform beyond your normal capabilities when engaged in it?

3. Is your energy level higher when engaged in it?

4. Do you get excited in anticipation of engaging in it?

5. Do you dream about the activity?

6. Is your enthusiasm for it consistent over time?

7. Do you feel more confident or empowered while engaged in it?

8. Do others notice you based on your involvement/performance in it?

9. Do others rally around you or want to be involved with you in the activity?

10. Do you feel energized after engaging in it?

PASSION IS WHO YOU ARE

Do not be overwhelmed by the suggestions I have made to you in this chapter. The most important thing you can remember when discovering your passion is that you are not creating something from nothing. Passion is already a part of you; your task is to expose it, to find the conditions that elicit it. The Romantic poet Samuel Taylor Coleridge acknowledged this, ironically in his poem entitled *Dejection: An Ode*.

It were a vain endeavor,

Though I should gaze forever

On that green light that lingers in the west:

I may not hope from outward forms to win

The passion and the life, whose fountains are within.

You cannot expect to magically conjure up passion in your life by focusing on things, on outward forms, that do not have resonance with or relevance to your heart. You can, however, take responsibility for discovering the conditions and circumstances that elicit your passion, that set the fountains flowing. When you understand your passion and what inspires it, you can commit to keeping it a vital part of your life. You can correct the mistake that so many of us have made and assume responsibility for your own happiness and success. You can make passion a central force in your life.

As you begin to seek out your passions, remember to make the following commitments.

Once you have uncovered your passions, or feel you have made a good start, move on to Step Three, which requires you to decide where you want your passion to lead you. Before doing so, use Worksheet #2 to document your process of discovery and your potential passions. Be sure to brainstorm

Passion Review

To discover my passions I will . . .
- Take a step back from my life
- Reflect and listen to my heart
- Look to my past, present, and future for clues as to what inspires and excites me
- Explore my passions once I identify them
- Seek inspiration by taking perspective breaks

some potential taste tests that will help you get in touch with your passion sooner rather than later. Do not feel that the lists you compile, both passions and taste tests, are written in stone. Part of following the Passion Plan is experimenting and learning. If you feel later on that you were mistaken in your suspicions or took an unproductive step in finding your passion, you can adapt your personal Passion Plan accordingly.

PASSION PLAN WORKSHEET #2

Step 2: Discover Your Passions   How

A. Passion(s) to Build into My Life:	What passion(s) have you discovered that you want to build into your life? Consider: • Discovery by epiphany • Discovery through change • Discovery through intuition • Discovery through experience Note: Remember to also consider several critical questions about your life when trying to discover your true passion, including: • Where am I today? • Where do I want to be tomorrow? • What do I regret in my life?
B. Potential Passion "Taste Tests" and Ways to Taste: 1.	Identify potential passions that you want to build back in to your life using a "taste-test" approach. In addition, list some potential ways to carry out your taste test.

Passion Plan Worksheet #2 (cont.)

**B. Potential Passion "Taste Tests"
and Ways to Taste (cont.):**

2.

Remember:
- These are passions that
  you want to begin
  building in to your life
  on your own terms
- Find nonthreatening
  ways to experience
  your passion

3.

4.

CHAPTER 5

Step Three
Clarify Your Purpose

"Would you tell me, please, which way I ought to go from here?"
"That depends a good deal on where you want to get to," said the Cat.
"I don't much care where—" said Alice.
"Then it doesn't matter which way you go," said the Cat.
"—so long as I get somewhere," Alice added as an explanation.
LEWIS CARROLL, *ALICE'S ADVENTURES IN WONDERLAND*, 1861

The first time I read *Alice's Adventures in Wonderland* and came across this passage, I thought how odd it would be for people to go through life like Alice went through her fantasy world, never knowing where they might end up. But as I grew older, I realized many of us do just that. We take things as they come, often making decisions based primarily on momentary concerns with little regard for present meaning or future impact. Certainly we end up somewhere, but probably not where we would if given a choice.

You are reading this book because, unlike Alice, you care about where you are going. You do have a choice. Just as we choose to live with passion, to follow our hearts, so must we decide what our passion means to us and where we want it to lead. We must have a *purpose* in pursuing it. Many people have discovered their passion but are unable to follow it with any sense of satisfaction because they do not take the time or effort to clarify what part it should play in their lives. This is tragic, because passion without purpose is meaningless.

Think of passion as a great river, teeming with energy. This energy can be unleashed in many ways and with many effects. It can escape unexpectedly and chaotically in the form of raging waves, rapid currents, and dangerous whirlpools, or be regulated wisely by careful channeling through a dam or levy. It can batter and destroy or nourish and renew. Your purpose is your dam. It is the conduit through which you harness your passion and use it toward positive ends. By establishing a purpose for your passion, you give yourself power over it. You, and you alone, can determine how you will use it, when you will use it, and where it will lead you.

CHANNELING YOUR PASSION

By now I hope you are in touch with your passion and have begun to feel its power. I hope that in these moments of peak experience you have also sensed the potential it offers to help you accomplish and achieve. Deciding how you want to use your passion is a serious choice but also an uplifting one. Think about it. It is almost as if you have found a treasure and must decide how you and the world will benefit from it. Will it make you and you alone rich, or will you spread your new-found wealth to others? Will you use it to increase your knowledge, improve your community, or help others? Will it complicate your life or simplify it, move you away from your current setting or tie you closer to it?

Answering these questions will require a great deal of thought and foresight. To help as you begin the process of clarifying your purpose, consider a woman we'll call Erin. Erin entered a top college unsure what to study or what career to pursue. During a freshman survey course in economics, she became intrigued by the workings of macro- and microeconomic systems. She got an "A" in the course and decided to sign up for a few more classes in the department. Erin eventually majored in economics, a choice that surprised her friends and family at home. To them economics seemed inconsistent with her caring, giving nature. She had always displayed great concern for those in need—physically, emotionally, or spiritually—and had spent much of her free time tutoring and volunteering in her community. She was passionate about the power of human potential and felt an overwhelming desire to show others how they could overcome their limitations. Her loved ones had assumed she would study medicine, education, or some other discipline that would allow her to help others directly. Economics did not seem to be one of them.

But Erin saw the potential in it for helping others. Besides, she felt excited whenever she cracked an econometrics text or attended a lecture on Keynesian theory. Although puzzled by her growing fascination with charts and graphs and equations, she knew that the abstractions she studied in the classroom represented real forces in the lives of real people. Recessions, depressions, and economic instability created hardship, which in turn created starving children, defeated parents, and failing societies. In learning about the forces that created these social ills, especially in the world's developing countries, she hoped to find ways to combat them.

Another consideration was purely pragmatic. Economics, with its inroads into banking and finance, offered perhaps the best opportunity for her to get a high-paying job. She had acquired a mountain of educational debt and would be repaying her student loans for many years. Her parents, though supportive, could offer her little money. She was committed to gaining financial security, something her family had never known. Motivated by her interest and driven by her desire to succeed, she studied with great intensity, earning nearly perfect grades, winning the respect of her professors, and heightening her commitment to the field.

Brimming with intelligence and enthusiasm, Erin landed a high-paying job with a Wall Street investment bank, an accomplishment commensurate with her university performance. She entered the world of mergers and acquisitions and learned everything there was to know about leveraged buyouts and hostile takeovers. She enjoyed her work, but found herself longing for a more altruistic role, something that would allow her to use her love of economics toward more socially productive ends. Little did she know that her then-latent passion for helping others would soon lead her away from a fast-paced metropolis to sleepy South American villages.

Erin returned to graduate school, where she enrolled in a joint degree program that would allow her to pursue both passions simultaneously. An MBA would further hone her expertise at dealing with finance at the institutional level, and a master's in international relations would address her desire to better understand the people she wanted to help, namely those of third-world countries. After completing her second year of classes she accepted a summer consulting position in Argentina. She was supposed to return after three months, but did not make it back for three and a half years. She fell in love with the country, the people, and the work she was doing there. Her assignment was to study how foreign capital could be used to provide economic opportunities for those who would otherwise be denied them. The entrepreneurial spirit her clients displayed amazed her. They had been taught from birth that they could not rise from poverty, but given the smallest of loans they were able to build entirely new lives through ingenuity, resourcefulness, and commitment. She was so inspired by their example and exhilarated by the part she played in it that she decided to devote her career to furthering such efforts.

Erin has since returned to the United States to work in the firm's headquarters, welcoming the opportunity to promote similar programs in other countries. In conjunction with her field research, she has written a book documenting the organization's work, highlighting the lessons they have learned, and offering suggestions for future work to other organizations. She is convinced that if the model she has helped to establish is replicated around the globe millions of lives will be improved and as many will be given the chance to claim the potential so many of us take for granted.

Erin is a wonderful example of using passion effectively. One key to her success has been clarity of purpose. Over the years she refined her passions and brought them into focus. She decided how she wanted to pursue them and why. Erin's purpose is not to make obscene amounts of money (although she certainly could have), nor is it to win awards or bring attention to herself (also a distinct possibility). It is to make a lasting contribution to the economic systems of developing countries and to improve the lives of their citizens. From the moment she realized that, her career centered on it. It clarified her passions and gave them direction.

UNDERSTANDING YOUR OPTIONS

Like Erin, once you've discovered your passions, you must decide where you want them to take you. What role will they play in your life? Will they become your livelihood, mere hobbies, or a perennial quest? Will they involve others or be something you do alone? Let's assume, for example, you have a passion for basketball. You might begin training for the NBA, learn to officiate, cover high school games for the local newspaper, or coach youngsters at the YMCA. Or, if your personal circumstances allow, you might even become a full-time fan, attending every professional, college, and middle-school game in your area.

The path you choose in this case probably depends on your situation. Are you a middle-aged father of three, a college student, or a retiree? Is money a concern? Are you free to travel? Chances are that unless you are a world-class athlete, the purpose basketball assumes in your life will be of a recreational rather than professional nature. Though as a father you might dream to play against the MVP of the NBA giants, reality dictates against it. Quitting your job, hiring a personal trainer, and working out round the clock would not change that. To follow your passion in such a direction without regard for the other things that are important to you would be irresponsible at best.

When you define a purpose for your passion, you reconcile it with reality. Not that passion isn't the stuff dreams are made of, because it is, and I am not suggesting that you can't achieve your dreams. But abandoning reality isn't going to help. To use your passion effectively, you must carefully consider and define your purpose.

You may question this, but I guarantee that those who are truly happy with their lives remain true not just to their passion but to their purpose. Poll the players of an NBA team, and you will find that no player's reason for joining the league was identical to another's. Most would probably profess a passion for the sport, but why they pursued it to such great lengths will vary. One might have done it to make his mother proud, another to earn $100 million before he's thirty, and yet another so that he could master the sport to his fullest potential. Others might have abandoned similar careers because they did not allow them to stay aligned with their purpose. One might have left because he viewed the costs to his health to be too great, another because it estranged him from family, and yet another because he could no longer perform to the standards he had set for himself.

ANTICIPATING OUTCOMES

As you let passion into your life, you will find that the best way to hold on to it is to set clear expectations for where you want it to lead. These can and probably will change over time, but if you keep them foremost in your mind they will help you stay focused on the outcomes you desire, on your Profit. The patterns of regret we follow often result from our failure to reconcile purpose and passion. A famous film director who often missed six months of his children's lives while shooting on location looks back and realizes his passion for filmmaking cost him memories he cannot recreate and experiences he cannot replace. A free spirit who spent decades pursuing his passion for travel comes to the sad realization that none of the friendships that were important to her have survived her extended absences. A powerful politician comes to the sad awareness that his obsession with power has obscured his passion for social progress. A supermodel wishes she could trade her fame and fortune for a life of humble anonymity.

As these examples clearly show, we often fail to anticipate the outcomes of following our passions. If you are going to bring passion into your life, understand that you are accountable for your choices. Be sure they reflect not only your passion but also what you really want in life, both in the short and long term. If I decide that above all I am passionate about teaching and want to devote my professional energies to the public school system, I must be aware what that entails. I will not get rich from my paychecks; if I want to retire rich, I will need to invest aggressively when young or simply choose another profession. If I take the time and energy to clarify my purpose before I begin, and possibly to adapt it as I go, then I will not end up kicking myself for my decision down the road.

I know a man who found himself in just this situation. He played professional baseball, but his career was cut short by illness and injury. He was passionate about his sport, and also about helping children. He became a high school coach and teacher and now, thirty years later, he is not sure if his time was worth the effort. Though he is grateful for the opportunity he had to touch the lives of many of his students, his

Passion Review

Before you begin building your life around your passion, decide
  where you want it to take you and determine the purpose it will
  fulfill. To do this you need to . . .

- Channel your passion
- Understand your options
- Anticipate possible outcomes

retirement income is not sufficient to meet his living expenses. He is now forced to work though officially he is retired. Ironically, the reason he continued teaching all those years was for the security his retirement plan would ostensibly provide. In so doing, he turned down many opportunities that could have led to more lucrative careers. Most days he regrets the choice he made to teach and wishes he had played out his passions in another way, perhaps by volunteering in his spare time or promoting sporting events to benefit children.

Passion should not be about living with regret, but rather about living without it. This is why clarifying your purpose is such a critical step in your personal Passion Plan.

WHAT IS YOUR PURPOSE?

To begin to clarify the direction your passions will take, look at your life and consider the concept of purpose in two lights.

The first is, "What is my purpose in the grand sense? What do I foresee my greatest possible accomplishments in life as being?" The second is, "Given my life as it is now, how can my passions help me to achieve this greater purpose? What specific purposes will they serve as I live from day to day?"

BIG PURPOSE

To begin, let's consider the first set of questions. Think about your purpose in life. What do you hope to accomplish? You have already asked yourself this question in the previous chapter, but as you ponder it now, think in terms of purpose. Focus not only on what you want to do, but on why.

Companies do this through mission statements. They express their objectives in a series of assertions that reflect the spirit of what the organization is trying to accomplish. For some it is first and foremost to earn a profit, for others it is to serve customers, to improve their industry, or to create an exciting workplace. The same is true of you. You can express your life mission in a series of similar phrases. For example, you might say, "My purpose in life is to build a strong and happy family, contribute to society, and find personal happiness." Your neighbor might claim his is to build a company, become expert in his field, and live life with gusto.

However you envision your life mission, I call it your "Big Purpose." It is your reason for being; it is your justification for living. Your Big Purpose, like your passion, stems from your heart. In fact, the two are closely if not inextricably linked. They work in tandem. Passioneers provide poignant examples of this fact.

I never had the opportunity to meet Mother Theresa, but as an admirer I speculate that she had a great passion for service. I also surmise, given her choice of career, that her Big Purpose was to serve her God by serving her fellow man. The choices that she made—to become a nun, to labor in the streets of Calcutta, and to serve as a spokeswoman for her cause—were no doubt inspired by her passion, but they were also informed by her purpose. She could have done many things with her passion—exercised it cautiously through weekend volunteering, reserved it exclusively for a husband and children of her own, or buried it altogether in favor of a materialistic, selfish existence. Because this passion was so central to her nature, however, I would argue that her Big Purpose emanated directly from it. In fact, it might be difficult to separate the two.

The same is true of countless others who have made lasting and significant contributions to the world. They are so intimately connected to their passion that it defines their Big Purpose. Most of us, however, do not fall in this category. We are pulled in conflicting directions by circumstance, the influence of others, self-doubt, and a hundred other forces that prevent us from seeing our Big Purpose. For us passion and purpose have become removed. Our challenge is to reconcile the two.

Probably you are musing over your own Big Purpose right now, wondering if you even have one. Don't be intimidated by the idea. Having a Big Purpose should not weigh you down with thoughts so momentous that you cannot enjoy life. It just means you view your life as significant. You see it as a progression of events and experiences leading to a meaningful end.

You might already be living your Big Purpose without knowing it. A common purpose that people often take for granted is building a family. So much of our lives are focused around our relationships with our parents, our siblings, our spouses, and our children that we forget they are a noble pursuit in and of themselves. The decisions you have made in your life may already reflect your commitment to your family: the jobs you have taken, the places you have lived, the people you have associated with. I know many people who, though proud of their personal and professional accomplishments, feel the value in such achievements is that they make them better, stronger family members. A father may accept an award from his peers because it shows his children the value of diligence and commitment to a profession. A young woman might do the same as recognition of the love and support her parents have given her over the years.

You might also unknowingly be pursuing a Big Purpose that centers purely on you. This may be true whether you feel fulfilled now or are struggling to make sense of your life. In fact, any dissatisfaction you may be feeling could stem from your inability to take decisive steps to work toward your purpose. If you fall into this category, your purpose could be to gain knowledge or skills, distinguish yourself in your work, or be the best you can in specific activities. For many of us our underlying Big Purpose has to do with personal improvement, but we are suppressed or stifled in some way—by unappreciative bosses, personal misgivings, or perceived limitations. We have a sense that we want to accomplish great things by improving ourselves, but we are not able to act on it aggressively.

Some of us have a Big Purpose centered on contributing to society: easing the burdens of others, making earth-shattering discoveries, saving the environment. Because addressing such concerns requires a great degree of involvement—they do not blend into the background as easily as our personal concerns—those who possess such purposes are often acutely aware of their importance. They must work actively and consciously to serve such ends, and do so with deep regard for bringing them about.

Possibly you do not feel an overriding sense of purpose, that you live for experience and not overtly for meaning. If so, your Big Purpose is to live a fulfilling life or to fill your life with experiences you view as worthwhile. Even if you fall into this category, your passion is relevant to building the life you want. In fact, if you are concerned primarily with experience, pursuing your passions seems an obvious source of fulfillment: when you engage your passion, you heighten the quality of your experience.

Regardless of how you view your Big Purpose, if at all, your passion is the most powerful tool you possess in fulfilling it. Passioneers understand this relationship and usually succeed in bridging the gap between the two. Most of us miss the connection completely and assume that fun and excitement have no place in our quest. This then becomes our challenge: using our passion to achieve our Big Purpose.

Let's go back to the example of someone whose Big Purpose is building a strong family. A father who views his profession first and foremost as a means of providing for his children might not put job satisfaction high on his list of priorities. As such, he might never realize that he could be happier and perhaps a more successful breadwinner if he pursued a career that reflected his passion. Similarly, an artist whose life mission is to create a masterpiece might never understand that her best prospect at achieving this is by following her passion in choosing materials, media, and subjects other than the current prescriptions of her field.

PASSION COMES FIRST

If you are confused about how passion relates to purpose, you are not alone. Until this point we have dealt purely with passion and I have argued that it should be at the center of your life. Purpose is related to passion but seemingly threatens to depose it from prominence. Which comes first? Do we define our purpose and then enlist our passion to accomplish it, or do we discover our passion and then define a purpose that imitates it? There is no easy answer, but I believe passion comes first because very often your purpose is a direct reflection of your passion. If, for example, you love helping others, your purpose will probably involve this passion. It might be to eliminate hunger, to teach children, or to empower the elderly. If you love to learn, your purpose will likely involve the knowledge you gain. It could be to teach others, to contribute to a chosen field, or to increase your understanding of the world. In this way, your purpose emanates from your heart, just as your passion does.

The difficulty arises when we consider our lives as we are living them today, not as they would be in an ideal world. Life often intervenes and distorts or conceals the desires of our heart. This is true for our purpose as well. You may have thought your great mission in life was to find a cure for cancer, but coming up with medical school tuition was too formidable a challenge. You might have felt your purpose was to explore the world and experience its many wonders and cultures, until fifteen years later you found yourself married with children who you cannot leave to make the journey.

There are innumerable reasons why the purpose that is natural to you is not the one you now pursue. Often they stem from abandoning passion. When life is out of synch with passion, the purpose that accompanies passion becomes irrelevant. In an ideal world, we could pick up our passions and run with them unhindered. The important people in our life would support us unconditionally, money would not be a concern, and responsibility would fade into the background. This is fantasy, however; life is firmly grounded in reality. Our purpose must therefore reflect the realm of the possible; mind you, I say possible, not necessarily probable. Teddy Roosevelt noted this when he said, "Keep your eyes on the stars, but remember to keep your feet on the ground."

This is such an important point I want to dwell on it a moment longer. The greatest danger in changing your life and embracing your passion is to ignore your current circumstances and drop everything, including many things that are important to you, in its pursuit. If you do, you will regret your choices and your passion will become a source of misery rather than joy. This is why purpose is so very important. You must have a sense of where you are now and what you hope to accomplish, what you are willing to sacrifice and what you hope to gain. Only when you feel comfortable in this knowledge can you begin to work passion into your life to your benefit.

History is also replete with people who have followed their passion to questionable and unfortunate ends. Popular accounts tell that Paul Gauguin abandoned his wife and children and a successful career as a stockbroker at the age of thirty-five to immerse himself in his art. We can assume that art was his passion, certainly. Gauguin denounced modern life for its hollowness and sought meaning and emotion in more primitive haunts. He traveled first to rural France and eventually to Tahiti, where he lived among the natives. His quest for truth in simplicity brought him great fame as an artist, yet apparently little solace on an emotional level. He attempted suicide, was unsuccessful, and died five years later a lonely man on an island in the Marquesas.

We cannot assume Gauguin regretted the choices he made. If his Big Purpose was to achieve fame, he accomplished it. If it was to make a notable contribution to the world of art, he succeeded. If he hoped to find truth through his art, perhaps he did, or he believed he did. But if part of his purpose was happiness, it appears he failed at that. He was so consumed by his passion that it led him to denounce many things that were integral to his emotional well-being.

KEY PROFIT AREAS

The point the Gauguin story demonstrates is that you must establish your purpose if you do not want to end up trading your passion for your happiness. Before you integrate passion into your life, you need to consider not only your Big Purpose but the smaller, equally important purposes you hope to fulfill in various aspects of your life. Implicit in any vision you might have of your future must be regard for your emotional, physical, and spiritual state; the nature of your relationships with others at home, at work, and in social settings; your intellectual growth; your financial condition; and your role as a member of society. These I call "key profit areas."

As described in earlier chapters, Profit is any result you are seeking in building a better life. It is what you long for, your pot of gold at the end of the rainbow. There may be one thing you value or want most, but you probably hope to achieve many things: good health, strong relationships, financial security, the respect of your colleagues. Your expectations in each key profit area are critical to building a successful passion-filled life. The changes that you make must reinforce rather than compromise your objectives. If you succeed in one area at the expense of another, you have not gained much.

At the end of the chapter you will map out your own key profit areas. To help you begin to see your life in this light— as a rubric of purposes—here are nine key profit areas and examples of Profit you might seek in each. As you review this list, consider what you want in each area and how your passion might help you achieve it.

Emotional—anything pertaining to the overall quality of your day-to-day experience as reflected by your moods and affective responses. Most people describe happiness or fulfillment as the emotional state they most desire; you probably seek them as well. Passion itself is another form of emotional Profit.

Spiritual—anything pertaining to your consciousness above and beyond the physical plane as reflected by your beliefs in deity or the metaphysical. Forms of spiritual Profit include increased faith, a sense of peace with the world and your place in it, and greater understanding of your individual potential.

Physical—anything pertaining to the condition of your body. Forms of physical Profit include increased strength, weight loss, and heightened performance in athletic events.

Interpersonal—anything pertaining to your relationships with others, including family members, friends, and acquaintances. Forms of interpersonal Profit include entering into marriage, building trust, and increasing communication.

Financial—anything pertaining to money. Forms of financial Profit include increased income, retirement from employment, and freedom from debt.

Professional—anything pertaining to employment or career. Forms of professional Profit include recognition by colleagues, job promotion, and contribution to a field or industry.

Intellectual—anything pertaining to thinking or knowledge. Forms of intellectual Profit include understanding of a new subject, fluency in a foreign language, and increased ability to express your thoughts through speech or writing.

Civic—anything pertaining to being a citizen or member of a community, city, state, or nation. Forms of civic Profit include camaraderie between neighbors, service to government and schools, and preservation of the environment.

Humanitarian—anything pertaining to the welfare of your fellow man. Forms of humanitarian Profit include improvement of the lives of others by meeting their financial, spiritual, or emotional needs.

For many reasons you need to recognize these Profit areas and their importance in your life. The danger in ignoring them and the purposes they inspire is not simply the possibility of going off the deep end, as Gauguin did. Few of us could ever go to such lengths, but we might retreat from the pool altogether. We err on the side of caution rather than abandon. We sense that we want certain things, but we are afraid to go after them. By acknowledging your purpose in these areas, you also acknowledge your right to achieve them.

PIECES OF THE PIE

Now that you have given some thought to these different areas, create a picture in your mind of how they work together to serve your Big Purpose. Though they may seem disparate in nature, in reality they share many of the same characteristics, not the least of which is that they are a direct manifestation of who you are. In fact these smaller purposes are closely connected because each and every one is essential to your fulfillment. Each is a piece of the pie that makes up your Big Purpose.

Because this is true, you will find that often when you fulfill one purpose you fulfill many. For example, if your purpose is to bring your body to peak condition, you might find that you also begin to expand your mind as you ponder life or discuss it with others on your five-mile training runs. These two accomplishments, achieved under the guise of a single activity, in turn might bring you closer to fulfilling your Big Purpose of making the most of the abilities you were born with, both physical and mental.

In embracing your passion, you will begin to see ways that the different things you do can serve your Big Purpose. Shakespeare recognized how seemingly disparate actions can serve a single end in this passage from *King Henry V* (1975 [1599], I, ii, 205):

Many things, having full reference

To one consent, may work contrariously;

As many arrows, loosed several ways,

Fly to one mark; as many ways meet in one town;

As many fresh streams meet in one salt sea;

As many lines close in on the dial's center;

So may a thousand actions, once afoot,

End in one purpose, and be all well borne

Without defeat.

The Bard may have been referring to different people accomplishing one objective in different ways. His words highlight the fact that our own actions, as unrelated as they may seem at times, can lead to a single desired end. This is true because, as he wrote, they emanate from a single consent—our hearts.

You can and should have many purposes in life, even if they seem at odds. They can, through planning and forethought, be achieved concurrently. Some may be more forthcoming than others, but none need be left out of your life. Together they paint a complete picture of who you are. Each is valuable; each is worthy of pursuit.

The diagrams in Figure 5.1a and 5.1b depict the many

Passion Review

Big Purpose   *Your life mission; your reason for living*

Key Profit Areas   *Different areas of your life for which you*
have specific, more immediate purposes.
They include but are not limited to the
following:

- Emotional
- Spiritual
- Physical
- Interpersonal
- Financial
- Professional
- Intellectual
- Civic
- Humanitarian

Your purposes in these areas are pieces in the pie of your
Big Purpose. Each contributes to it, though some might have
greater importance than others.

purposes of two men, both of whom seek to fulfill the same
Big Purpose—build a strong and happy family—but who
define it in very different ways. The unique visions of their
key profit areas and their relative importance in their lives
will determine the ways they will follow their passions as well
as the results they create.

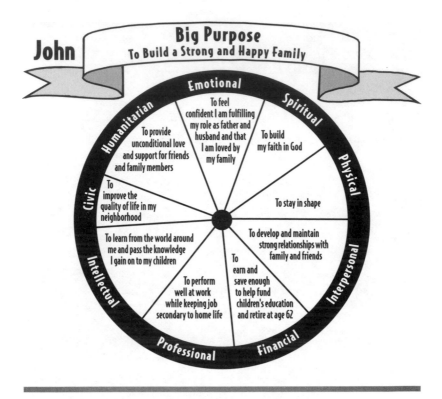

Figure 5.1a. Purpose Pie Chart Example.

A PURPOSE TO YOUR PASSION

The question then becomes how you are going to use your passion to pursue and achieve these purposes. As mentioned,
passion is the key to accomplishing your greatest desires, but
it needs to be used wisely. So the first step in putting your passion to work is not to unleash it but to determine how and to
what end it can serve you. This is the second aspect of purpose. You know your passion (or are beginning to) and you
know what you want in life, so how are you going to reconcile

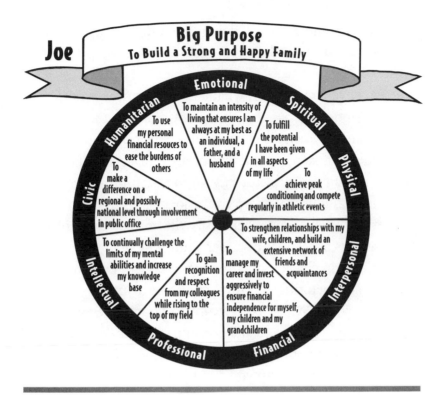

Figure 5.1b. Purpose Pie Chart Example.

the two? How can you ensure that your passion will work to your ultimate benefit?

This is where the thinking aspect of purpose comes into play. Although Big Purpose might emanate from your heart, the specific purposes you ascribe to your passions must be carefully reasoned and well thought out. This is true whether you are timid or bold. If you are reluctant or afraid to embrace your passion, defining the role it will play helps you accept and prepare for its presence in your life. If you are ready to give your life over to passion (something all of us dream of at one time or another), clarifying the purpose it will serve ensures you do not abuse or misuse this most precious of assets.

We have already seen what can happen if you neglect to take this step. Your passion, though bringing you great excitement and energy, can also bring you heartache and regret. And if we do not assign it some importance or accept its significance, passion can fizzle or fade against the pressures of our busy life. You must therefore give priority to passion by giving it purpose. This is true whether it will be the center of your life, a serious avocation, or a mere amusement.

So, looking back to your purpose model, how do you see your passion factoring in? How can it best help you to achieve what you want? Will it be relevant to your professional life? Could it help you in your relationships with friends and family? Will it affect your spiritual well-being? Could you use it to earn a living? Can it help you feel better about yourself physically or intellectually?

As you think in these terms, look for possibilities rather than limitations. Think creatively. Look for ways in which your passion could come into play that might be unexpected or unique. If, for example, you have a passion for cooking, consider new ways to use that passion. You could feed your passion *and* help others by volunteering at the soup kitchen. You could strengthen family relationships by sharing your passion with your children—preparing meals together, baking gifts for friends and neighbors. You could possibly fulfill your entrepreneurial dreams by opening a restaurant, starting a catering business, or publishing a cookbook. Or you could simply keep cooking a private passion, indulging only when time and opportunity allow.

For each passion you can name, list all the purposes you believe it might serve. Then think about which of them you are prepared to accept and pursue. Given your current status—emotional, financial, and otherwise—what role do you think you are prepared to give this passion in your life? Are you ready to work it into your career? Can you see yourself pursuing it full-time, part-time, or only rarely? Are you willing to make sacrifices to pursue it? Will it require you to make significant changes or can you follow it without significantly altering your current situation?

After you have answered these questions, you should have a sense of the task that lies before you. The purpose you define now will determine the direction your passion will take. Certainly this direction can change as your purpose and priorities might change, but now it provides a starting point for bringing passion into your life.

Consider Marty, a forty-seven–year-old insurance broker from Minneapolis. He has been selling policies for more than twenty years, is respected by clients and colleagues, earns good money, and is generally pleased with his career. As a young man, Marty loved college but opted not to enter graduate school when his wife became pregnant with their first child. Recently, however, after taking a night-school class he rediscovered his passion for learning.

In considering how this passion will factor into his life, Marty might view it in a number of lights. He might deem it an indulgence—something he can pursue periodically through similar classes when time and money allow. He could consider it valuable in his current career path, and begin to move into a developmental role in his company. He might attend seminars, conduct research, and make suggestions regarding the future of his industry. If he wants to pursue his passion more ardently, he might decide to transition to another field, or, in the extreme, quit his job and return to graduate school.

The purpose Marty chooses will reflect his current situation and his larger life purpose. Given that his two sons will be entering college in the next few years, he might not feel it practical to abandon the security of his job. But if he were without an income and paying his own tuition, his children might find scholarships or receive financial aid to cover the expenses he could not. The middle path, and probably the most realistic, would be to work aggressively to bring his passion into his work while also pursuing it in night school. This would allow Marty to nurture and enjoy his passion while fulfilling his larger purpose of providing a college education for his children.

If Marty were miserable in the insurance business, or if he felt there was no flexibility in his current environment, he could take more drastic measures to bring passion back into his life—change jobs, make arrangements to begin graduate school. But because he is relatively satisfied and has room for his passion to reenter in less threatening ways, he would be best served by the less radical course. The fact that the changes he might make are subtle in no way undermines their importance. The easiest path would be for Marty to change nothing, to remember his college days fondly and think about what he might have become if he had continued in school. By assigning his passion a purpose of importance and growth, extending into his professional, recreational, and personal worlds, he ensures that if the time comes for him to make a more pronounced change, he will be prepared.

Marty's example might not seem so simple if things were more complicated—if, for example, his marriage were in trouble, or one of his sons required special medical care. What if his boss were unwilling to help him change his role, or if he owned the agency and could not change focus without bringing down the business? What if he were independently wealthy and could afford to send his entire town to graduate school? Suppose he felt a great sense of urgency to his passion that he must make every change possible to accommodate it?

Our lives are not one-dimensional and so neither will deciding what to do with our passion. If, however, you keep an eye on your Big Purpose you will be able to steer your course and end up where you really want to be.

RECONCILING YOUR PURPOSES

Jack and Heather grew up in beach communities. They both discovered a passion for volleyball in youth and followed that passion in similar ways. Heather began playing when she was ten, following the example of an older sister who began playing a few years earlier. She recalls that her natural ability brought her attention and respect most girls her age did not receive and fueled her progress in the sport. Jack was born into a family of volleyball devotees but surprisingly did not begin playing seriously until he was in high school. Because his family lived in a town where there was no high school team, his parents arranged for him to live with friends in a neighboring community.

Both Jack and Heather excelled in their chosen sport and continued to play in college. Heather married, and after graduating began playing on the beach circuit. Because she lived near the beach and wanted to continue competing, this seemed a logical way for her to continue to pursue her passion. Around this time she also began a career in banking, but she spent all her free time practicing and playing in tournaments. Jack sat out his freshman year on the team to retain his eligibility in a fifth year of college, then played on the varsity team for three years. In his final year, he began coaching and also turned to the beach circuit. He wanted to build a career around volleyball, and to do this he had to generate winnings.

Jack and Heather competed at tournaments for years before their paths finally crossed at an out-of-state competition. Heather had won the women's State Amateur title, and Jack had won the men's. Play at the tournament had been delayed by rain and the players gathered in a beachfront restaurant to pass the time. Heather bumped into Jack and asked him if he would sign her scrapbook, in which she had been documenting her travels and competitions. She recalls their first meeting with great fondness. As she handed Jack the book a friend snapped a picture of the pair, thereby recording the moment they first laid eyes on one another. They often look at the photograph and remember their encounter with destiny.

At that moment, if you had asked Heather her purpose in playing volleyball, she would have provided a surprising response. Though she began competing as a way to keep volleyball a vital part of her life, she continued for other reasons. At the time she met Jack her marriage was in trouble. Her husband, many years her senior, did not want children. She did, badly. To escape her problems, she immersed herself in volleyball. Every moment she was not at work, she was training or competing. If she focused on volleyball, she did not have to think about her marriage.

Not surprisingly, when Heather's purpose in playing changed she lost her excitement for the sport. She became a self-proclaimed burnout. The energy and enthusiasm she had once felt turned to exhaustion and disdain. She endured competitions only because they kept her away from home and her problems.

Jack, whose immediate purpose in following his passion was to keep it alive by building a career, was encountering similar frustrations. He loved the sport, that would not change. He did not, however, love the environment in which he was pursuing it. A strong member of a Christian church, Jack found the moral environment of the beach circuit disheartening. The drugs, the alcohol, and the backstabbing between competitors were almost more than he could bear. He began to question if this was the best way for him to pursue his passion.

When Jack and Heather returned home they continued the friendship that had budded at the tournament. They began competing together and learned that they enjoyed volleyball for many of the same reasons. By training and playing together, they were able to keep their passion for the sport alive despite the forces that had been working to kill it. In this way, part of their purpose in playing became spending time with one another—not in a romantic sense, but as kindred spirits.

A few years later Heather and her husband divorced. As she recovered from the heartache, she realized that Jack shared not only her passion for volleyball but also her passion for children and a strong family life. As the months passed, they learned more about their common beliefs and desires and fell

Passion Review

To clarify my purpose I will . . .
- Seek to understand my passion and where I want it to lead me
- Define my Big Purpose by deciding what is most important to me
- Determine the things that matter most in the different areas of my life
- Begin to look for ways that my passion can help me achieve my purposes

in love. They married shortly thereafter and their first daughter was born a year after they were married.

Parenthood forced them to reevaluate the purpose volleyball served in their lives. Jack was still coaching at the collegiate level but was discouraged by his salary and his opportunities for advancement. His first priority was to support his young family, and he quickly realized volleyball could not fulfill this need. He took a marketing job to pay the bills but was not willing to give up his involvement in coaching. By working from 6 A.M. to 3 P.M. at the office, he could make the trek across town to the university in time to supervise afternoon practice before returning home to Heather and the baby.

During her pregnancy and in the months following the birth, Heather accompanied Jack on weekends to the beach where they had been playing volleyball with a group of friends for fun. The purpose volleyball had assumed for her, given the recent changes in her life, was recreational. She still was passionate about the sport, but her reasons for participating had changed. In the absence of the pressure and negative energy she felt from competition, she could once again enjoy playing. It also provided for socializing with their friends.

When Heather became pregnant with her second child, she curtailed play again but continued to attend the weekend gatherings with Jack. Socializing was still fun for her, and as a bonus they could spend time together with their daughter. After play was over, they took her down to the shore to play in the ocean, to the marine discovery center under the pier, or to the boardwalk to ride the carousel. Though volleyball was not a part of these activities, it was the impetus that prompted them to start what has since become a family tradition.

Now, as the busy and proud parents of two wonderful little girls, Heather and Jack have found yet another purpose to their passion. When they play on weekends, they view their time together as a date—something they don't often get otherwise. As the children play under the supervision of friends they gain welcome release from the pressures of their daily lives and an opportunity to have fun together. They have competed once as a couple since becoming parents, but when I marveled at that Heather reminded me that competition has marked the demise of many a couple!

When I asked her if volleyball was indeed a passion for her, she quickly cited her former burnout and the fact that she is not competitive today. When I asked her if she could see herself living without volleyball, however, her response was an immediate no. Though she is not eager to compete again, she does plan to continue playing recreationally as long as her body will allow.

Heather's initial reaction reflects the misconception of many of us: that we are not truly passionate about something unless we are pursuing it intensely. Volleyball *is* a passion for both Heather and Jack. The purpose this passion has served has changed over the years to reflect the path they are following toward achieving their Big Purpose: to build a strong and loving family. Together they have found ways to make their passion serve this end and at the same time bring them much happiness. Jack is seeking new part-time coaching opportunities to feed his passion at another level, but knows his happiness does not depend on a professional association with the sport. Once the children are older, he and Heather hope to share their passion with others by opening a volleyball camp for beginners, but until then they are thrilled to be playing for their own enjoyment.

Heather and Jack have learned what so many of us never do—passion can help us achieve more and be happier. You may not consider their example glamorous or remarkable, but it offers truth. Their passion has been a valuable tool in building and keeping the life they want. It keeps them vital; it feeds their personal fulfillment; one could even contend it makes them better parents. They understand that though it often seems easier to drop our passions or forget them for a while, it is well worth the fight to keep them alive. Most important they recognize the importance of purpose—of knowing what they want and how their passion can help them achieve it.

I hope that after reading this chapter you have a sense of where you want to go with your passion and what it can do for you. Use Worksheet #3 to help you name the results you are seeking and the reasons you are seeking them. Be sure to identify your Big Purpose (as best you can) and list ways you feel your passion can help you fulfill it. Then list the outcomes you wish to find in the different areas of your life. Once you have completed the worksheet, you will be ready to move on to Step Four, where you will define the specific actions to take in pursuing your passion.

PASSION PLAN WORKSHEET #3

Step 3: Clarify Your Purpose	How
A. My "Big Purpose" in Life:	Define what you see as your primary purpose or mission in life. Like passion, your Big Purpose should stem from your heart as well. Some questions to consider when defining your Big Purpose include: • What is the most important accomplishment for me to achieve in my lifetime? • What difference do I want to make in this world? • What do I see as my life's work? • What do I want to be most remembered for accomplishing?
B. Ways My Passion(s) Can Help Me Achieve My Big Purpose: 1. 2.	Identify ways that the pursuit of your passions can help you achieve your Big Purpose. Look for possibilities, rather than limitations, of how your passions can work together to serve your Big Purpose. Some questions to consider when deciding how passion factors in:

Passion Plan Worksheet #3 (cont.)

B. Ways My Passion(s) Can Help Me Achieve My Big Purpose (cont.):

3.

4.

- How will I ensure that my passion will work to my ultimate benefit?
- Do any of my passions need to be combined?
- How do I see my passions factoring in to achieving my Big Purpose?
- What are some unique ways my passions might be carried out?

C. "Profit" I'd Like to Experience from My Passion Pursuits:

Category   Specific Examples

List the major categories and specific examples of how you would like to Profit from your passion pursuits. Some categories to consider include:

- Emotional
- Spiritual
- Physical
- Interpersonal
- Financial
- Professional
- Intellectual
- Civic
- Humanitarian

CHAPTER 6

Step Four
Define Your Actions

We never know how high we are
Till we are called to rise
And then, if we are true to plan
Our statures touch the skies.
EMILY DICKINSON, 1870

By now you may be ready for action, to make your move. You have listened to your heart, considered your purpose, and are prepared to set off on the road to your personal Profit. Before you begin blazing your passion trail, however, I want to ask you one simple question. When the rubber meets the road, in which direction will you be headed? If, in the excitement of change, you speed off with a destination in mind but no idea how to get there, it is hard to predict where you might end up. You need a road map for results, a plan of action that will ensure you are actually moving toward your Profit rather than away from it.

In this chapter I will show you how to define the actions you will take to reorient your life around passion. You will create an action plan, your own step-by-step strategy for change and growth. You will plan both the steps you will take to let passion in and the ways you will nurture and strengthen it once it is present. You will envision possible scenarios and prepare to handle the outcomes you expect as well as those you do not. Most important, you will outline the paths that offer the best opportunity for reaching your Profit without threatening your happiness or commitment.

Your action plan will be unique because your passion is unique and so is your current situation. Many things will determine the shape it takes, including your present obligations, your willingness to sacrifice, and your feelings about your life today. You may need to plan major changes or only minor adjustments. Perhaps you can make these changes today; maybe you would prefer to introduce them gradually. If passion is already present in your life, you may need only to focus your efforts. If passion is new to you, you might need an overhaul, changing not just your activities but also your perception of your life.

Regardless, your action plan will be the starting point for building a new, passion-filled life. It articulates where you are, where you want to be, and how you imagine getting there. It is an attempt to connect visions of the future with conditions of the present, a blueprint for putting your passion to work.

SCOPE, INTENSITY, AND PACE

Before you put your action plan to paper, listen to your heart once again. How distant does the life you want to live seem? Are you happy with things now and simply want to achieve more, or are you so frustrated that you want to change everything? How willing are you to change, and how fast? What do you need to change today, and what can wait until tomorrow? Where is passion missing in your life, and how can you get it back?

The answers you provide determine your scope, intensity, and pace—the three characteristics that will define your action plan. Let's look at them more closely.

Scope

In the previous chapter you concentrated on the emotional, spiritual, physical, interpersonal, financial, professional, intellectual, civic, and humanitarian aspects of your life. Passion may be present in some of these areas but completely absent in others. You may feel fulfilled in your relationships with your loved ones but sense something is missing in your career. You might have a strong sense of spiritual purpose and identity but feel you are not living up to either. In crafting your action plan, you need to decide which aspects of your life to target for action and therefore what scope it will assume. I am a firm believer in the maxim, "If it ain't broke, don't fix it." If your passion is alive and thriving in certain areas, then by all means don't interfere with it. Do, however, seek to develop and enrich it. You might also make changes in other aspects of your life that might support it or help it to spread. Likewise, if you feel that something is stifling your passion in a given area, plan to make changes that will unleash it. The scope of your action plan should include each aspect of your life on some level. As you begin, however, you might feel more comfortable addressing only a few key areas. Only you can determine the scope of your plan. Whether it addresses all areas or only one, it is critical that you make a commitment to focus on these areas and work to bring passion into them.

Intensity

You are innately aware of what you can handle at any given time. Certainly you can surprise yourself, though, and when passion comes into play you are capable of more than you might imagine. When creating your action plan, however, have a sense of the intensity with which you can begin to pursue passion. If you are spread too thin as it is, with much energy devoted to the needs of others—coworkers, friends, family—the ardor with which you approach your passion might be less than that of someone less involved. But as passion creeps in, your intensity will naturally increase. Be optimistic and enthusiastic at the outset, but also be frank with yourself. Approach your passion at an intensity that feels comfortable but that also challenges you. If you pursue it with more energy than you have to give, you might end up abandoning it altogether.

Pace

This is similar to intensity but indicates a commitment of time rather than energy. As you develop your plan, you might set ambitious goals that you want to achieve quickly. This might lead you to make immediate and pronounced changes in your life—quit your job, move, surround yourself with different people. Or you might want to take things slowly and become more familiar with your passion and the ways it can work in your life. You might devote a few hours per week to learning more about it or becoming more skilled at it. Your pace, of course, can change over time. As you nurture your passion even in the smallest ways, you will begin to see alternatives. With the self-knowledge you gain, you might decide to speed up your pursuit or slow it down. Regardless, if you are confident in and committed to your passion you will begin to feel its effects.

The correlation between scope, intensity, and pace is usually direct. In other words, when people are prepared to make sweeping changes their scope is broader, intensity higher, and pace faster. When they are cautious about it their scope is narrower, intensity lower, and pace slower. This is not always the case, and you alone can determine your need and readiness for change.

To help you begin, place yourself in one of the following categories:

- Aggressive: ready to aggressively pursue your passion by making rapid and sweeping changes in your life
- Moderate: ready to devote considerable energy to pursuing your passion by making successive and significant changes in many areas of your life
- Reserved: prepared to pursue your passion by making gradual yet progressive changes in at least one area of your life

The category you select is a guideline for creating your action plan. The changes you target should thus be consistent with it. If, for example, you are reserved, planning for broad change in the near future would be foolish. By the same token, if you are aggressive, slating few and narrow changes might rob you of enthusiasm or commitment.

Passion Review

Your scope, intensity, and pace factors determine the approach you should take in developing your action plan:

- Scope means the breadth of your action plan; it reflects how many areas of your life it entails.
- Intensity is the force of your action plan; it reflects how much time and energy it requires.
- Pace is the speed of your action plan; it reflects the rate of change it presumes.

DEVELOPING AN ACTION PLAN

Using scope, intensity, and pace as a guide, you are ready to develop an action plan to define the steps you will take to make passion a permanent force in your life. Use Worksheet #4 at the end of the chapter to help you. You might want to copy it so you can jot down your ideas as you read, or you can choose to fill it out after you have finished the chapter.

As the worksheet indicates, the action plan has three basic components: the long-term plan, the short-term plan, and the contingency plan. The long-term plan provides an overall picture of the changes you want to make as well as a schedule for making them. The short-term plan reflects specific and immediate actions you will take to bring these changes about. The contingency plan helps you to keep moving forward if things turn out differently than you expect.

Start by creating the long-term plan. This might seem odd, but a solid vision of the future helps decide what steps to take now. Move on to contingency plans in case your long-term plan has to change. Finally create a short-term plan, your final preparation before you begin to act on your passion.

Long-Term Planning

In previous chapters you identified your passions and your purposes in pursuing them. These provide a picture of the future you want. What major changes will bring this future about? Will they occur over five, ten, twenty years? Your long-term plan is an acknowledgment that significant change takes time no matter what. You can embrace new passions wholeheartedly today, but the goals you seek may take a day, a month, a year, or much longer to meet. Passion is valuable and should be treated as such, which means we cannot hope to just turn it on and watch it go. We should think about it, nurture it, and develop it over the course of a lifetime.

My long term plan has been critical to the evolution of my passions and to the ways I have made day-to-day decisions. I chose to play out my entrepreneurial passion over time. The lemonade stand was gratifying, but I needed to learn about life, refine my skills, build my contacts, and increase my knowledge to give myself the best shot at success. Wanting to start a business was not enough. I had to plan.

Almost everything I have done since college—graduate studies, work experience, involvement in professional and volunteer organizations—has been a step in my long-term plan. All of them in some way influenced me and shaped the entrepreneur I am today and that I hope to be in the future. As my business grows, I continue to plan by making short-term decisions based on their long-term impact. I still seek to build skills and experiences that will enable the company to build future success.

To create a long-term plan, consider your goals—the purposes you want to fulfill in your life—and then assign an interval for achieving them. If your passion is travel, your goal might be to have the freedom and money to explore the globe at will. If you are thirty-five and in a budding career, you need patience and planning. You could follow many paths to realize your dream, but each would involve a unique plan. Your options might include the following:

Retire young. Probably you would have to sacrifice now to save money to travel later. You might create five-, ten-, and fifteen-year plans for saving and investment. This in turn might affect how you view your career and your goals in moving it forward. You might decide to take a new job if you are not promoted within a certain period or to begin training so you can make a change to a more lucrative field.

Pursue a new career that involves travel or lets you work from anywhere. This might not give you the freedom you desire now, but it may be the best way to achieve your goal. To do it could mean setting a five-year goal for finding and moving into the field and a ten-year goal for distinguishing yourself in it. Depending on the field you choose, you might set midterm goals of founding a travel agency, publishing travel articles, or building an international clientele.

Plan to study geography, culture, or languages at retirement. Holidays and vacations could help feed your passion until then.

Choosing any such course of action is a significant step in reaching your goal. Taking a safari in ten years might seem like a pipe dream, but when it is part of your plan you begin to make it a reality. Will you make the trip happen if you tell yourself you'll go "someday," or if you say, "I'm going in three years"?

Exactly how you will accomplish a long-term plan might not be evident. If I say my long-term goal is to build a business, then attending business school or working five years in someone else's business might be pieces of my plan. But if my focus is not on building new skills but rather on discovering what new business to start, it could take three years of research and experimentation. What will come out of that I cannot know, but I do know how long I want to investigate.

You can set milestones according to your preferences. If you prefer, measure your accomplishments in terms of time and view them as phases in your life. Using the previous example, you might plan for a research period before starting your business but not assign specific time in which to complete it. You also might mark your milestones by major life events such as marriage or retirement. If one of your goals is to find a partner and get married, it is unlikely you can make it happen simply by professing that you intend to get married by thirty-five. But you can predicate changes on an event if and when it occurs. Not that you won't pursue your passion if you do not get married, but you might do it differently.

Contingency Planning

This sort of situation is why developing contingencies is important for both your short- and long-term plans. Because the future is uncertain, and because the outcomes of your efforts are not always predictable, you need contingency plans. When I joined the professional bowlers' tour, I achieved one of the goals in my long-term plan. I soon discovered, however, that it was not that important to me. I enjoyed the bowling, but that only took a few hours a day. The rest was traveling, motel rooms, and hanging out. I had time on my hands that I could not fill in any meaningful or productive way. I remained on the tour for only six months. After that I continued to compete, but only at tournaments near my home when I was not working or studying.

That was my back-up plan if the bowling tour did not work for me, for whatever reason: return to school. Without that contingency in place I might have felt compelled to stay on the tour, and what had started as a passion-inspiring activity could have become passion-draining.

Many executives I have counseled over the years fall into this trap. They climb the corporate ladder and finally get the dream job they always hoped for. Instead of enjoying their success, however, they are miserable. Either they have changed or the job was not what they expected, but they find themselves longing for something different. Unfortunately few are brave enough to leave. They find it hard to relinquish what they worked so hard to get. But if they had prepared themselves for this possibility, if they had planned for it, it would not be so hard to make a change.

Contingency planning is crucial because you cannot predict your feelings any more than you can the events that inspire them. By working different scenarios into your plan, you will be better prepared to handle the surprising or the unexpected. You will also recognize that though your plan provides a guideline, it is not written in stone. It can lead you in different directions depending on your responses and the responses of the world. If you don't like something, you don't have to stick with it. If others don't appreciate or reward you for your efforts, you have other options. The only element of the plan that must remain fixed is passion. It is the core, the center from which all your possibilities emanate.

Short-Term Planning

Once your long-term and contingency plans are in place, you are ready to look to the short term. How will you begin today, tomorrow, or next week to make the changes that will help you achieve your long-term goals? Which changes take highest priority? What steps can you take now to ensure that you will bring passion into your life in a strong and meaningful way?

There are three steps to take in devising your short-term plan:

1. Move away from passion depleting experiences.
2. Introduce passion-inspiring experiences.
3. Become an executor, not a dreamer.

Without doing these in the short term, your long-term plan does not stand a chance.

Move Away from Passion-Depleting Experiences
You must take immediate action to integrate your passion into your life, but moving passion in probably requires moving something else out. As part of your short-term plan, target

whatever drains you of energy and leaves you frustrated or unhappy. Seek to improve or eliminate those factors, because it is hard to embrace passion if you are too depleted to enjoy it.

If your job drains you of passion, it is a difficult dilemma. Most of us must work. It is a financial imperative. So leaving a job usually means planning for a gradual change. Even if we are not prepared to quit, we can take immediate steps to make our work situation more bearable, perhaps even enjoyable. If you are in this situation, the first thing you can do is change your attitude toward your job. If job change is part of your long-term plan, view your current position as a mere step in your passion progression, a temporary lesson in what to avoid. Knowing that you are planning and taking steps to move on can make your remaining time less painful.

If you want to stay with your job, plan to make changes that bring passion into your work. Try to change your responsibilities by taking on a new position or changing the focus of your current one. Work with different people by joining different teams or departments, if possible. Look for new challenges or approach old ones with a different focus. Some of these might happen by chance, but planning for them makes them more likely. So your short-term plan might include meeting with your boss to discuss opportunities, working extra hours to facilitate a transition between positions, or researching possibilities for change on your own.

If your job does not present a threat to your passion, other activities or people in your life might. Ironically, you might be doing things that you think are important but that belie your true feelings. Perhaps you work out at the gym three nights a week to stay in shape physically but leave feeling strained emotionally. Despite your efforts to convince yourself otherwise, perhaps you loathe weight training. Maybe you are uncomfortable in the meat-market atmosphere or resent the attitude of your personal trainer. Your emotional depletion could result from any number of causes, and your plan must provide a way to counteract them. In this case you have many options: quit the gym, join another one, hire a new trainer, or take up swimming instead. The action you choose will depend on the source of your frustration and the potential for passion offered by the change.

Introduce Passion-Inspiring Experiences

As you plan to move the detrimental out of your life, plan also to move the beneficial in. If you have a passion for toys and your long-term plan is to design and manufacture them, your short-term plan for letting this passion into your life might be making regular visits to the local toy store or keeping a journal of your sketches and ideas. These small activities provide the backdrop for the subsequent steps in your plan, which might include taking design classes, consulting lawyers and accountants regarding business requirements, learning about materials, and manufacturing prototypes.

If you had a newly discovered passion for dance, you might plan to one day join a performing group or start your own studio. Before you could do that, however, you would need to pursue your passion at a more immediate level, perhaps by training and taking classes. You might also attend performances and visit other studios. Eventually you could audition for troupes or recruit teachers as your long-term goal grows nearer. The latter steps are critical to your success, but they are not possible if you do not take the first steps. Without them your passion would remain outside reality—a passion only in your dreams.

Become an Executor, Not a Dreamer

By translating a dream into action, you take a step that so many never do. You become not just a dreamer but an executor. You take control of your dreams rather than leaving them to the mercy of chance. Your short-term plan lays the groundwork for letting your passion in and then moving forward with it. Bearing this in mind, when you put your short-term plan to paper, begin by listing steps that you know you are prepared to take. If you aim too high too soon, you might be tempted to fall away from your plan.

You might have experienced this phenomenon once or twice when embarking on an exercise or diet plan. You begin, committed to seeing it through, but find it too much to handle. The same with New Year's resolutions: we set our ideals as immediate goals, forgetting that we need to build up to them; we cannot merely write them down and watch them materialize.

Your short-term plan should reflect your willingness to act as well as acknowledge the steps involved in getting there. Plan to work passion into your life in meaningful ways that you are prepared to accept. Do not demand too much of it too quickly. Down the road, as you carry out your long-term plan, you will need to challenge yourself and sometimes step outside your comfort zone to further develop your passion, but in the short term you need to ensure only that you begin. After all, if you give up tomorrow or next month because your short-term plan is too ambitious or unrealistic, your long-term plan will be irrelevant.

I don't want to suggest, however, that you should not be ambitious and even aggressive in your initial pursuit. Just as your short-term plan should not demand too much, it should not demand too little. Being an executor means taking action. If the steps you take are not significant, if they are perfunctory gestures instead of definitive acts, they will not be sufficient to change your life. Your passion will remain on the periphery rather than at the center of your existence.

PLANNING FOR SUCCESS

Susan, who has a self-proclaimed passion for words, is in the early stages of carrying out her action plan. She loves to read, write, and reason with words. We all use words, but to Susan they are things of beauty, the lens through which she views and interprets life. With them she can create images, elicit emotions, and sway opinions. When it came time for Susan to choose a profession, she thought the law presented an exciting opportunity for her to use words in a pragmatic way. She could make a living by using words to persuade clients, juries, and judges. She entered law school eager to learn and even more eager to write and to argue. Surely she would be a natural.

What came to her, though, was not the excitement she had anticipated but dread. She was in the wrong place. The words she felt stirring inside her were the stuff of fiction, not of torts and injunctions. There was a novel brewing inside her! She met a lawyer who had published a novel and discussed her dilemma with him. She felt she couldn't quit law school after she had invested so much time and money in it, but she also couldn't write novels while she was devoted full-time to the law. Instead of empathizing, he opened her eyes to some options.

He told Susan that completing her degree added value to any writing career she might build. A JD would give her instant credibility and a basis of experience and insight. Susan was not sure she wanted to pay the bills with her writing, only that she had to write because she wanted to. At the lawyer's suggestion, she began to devote one hour a day to writing. She was worried that applying discipline to her newfound passion might strain it, but instead it thrived. Her dread evaporated. The euphoria she felt while writing was enough to carry her through classes and even her late night study sessions. She describes her writing as "an incredibly vivid experience" that added a new level of fulfillment to her days.

Susan continued to write after graduating but did so purely for enjoyment. She took a job with an environmental law firm and eventually moved on to a firm that specialized in employment law. She did not enjoy the work but was proud of her professional accomplishments. As in law school, the hour per day she devoted to writing helped her endure. As time passed, she completed her first novel and then began a second. Staring at the manuscript one night, she realized that perhaps she was not doing this just for herself. Maybe she could share the fruits of her passion with others. She sent a copy to an agent a friend had recommended, but immediately regretted it. She became depressed because she was sure that rejection was going to be far worse than the uncertainty of never applying.

Susan was shocked when the agent offered to represent her. He loved the book and thought it showed great promise.

This is the moment that planning came into play for Susan. She felt she had come to a crossroads. She loved writing. There was no question about that. She was growing increasingly unhappy with her work because it was not fulfilling in either a creative or productive sense. She had become disillusioned and was also finding it harder and harder to set aside her daily hour as the pressure to perform at work intensified. She knew something had to change. But how and when?

Susan sat down one night and gave the matter serious thought. She pondered what she loved about writing and how she could keep it a constant in her life. One possibility was to write full time. This did not seem viable because she needed a steady income to make her student loan payments. (Her agent thought he could sell her manuscript, but wanted to wait until the market was more receptive to action thrillers, her chosen genre.)

The most reasonable and likely possibility for Susan was to continue her hour-per-day writing and find a less demanding job, probably outside law. Working in another field would not bother her because, she told me, "as long as I take that hour for myself, then I have the energy to go out and work for someone else." She also knew that she needed more than writing because it was too isolating to do exclusively.

Susan created both a long-term and short-term plan to help her build her life around her passion. Her eventual goal was to become a published novelist and earn enough money at writing that she could pay off her loans and have greater freedom in choosing when and where she would work. Her long-term plan included milestones for completing future novels and refining her craft. To do any of this, however, she had to take immediate action. Her short-term plan dictated that she begin looking for another job, possibly at a nonprofit organization or as a speechwriter. Surprisingly, she felt she had to eliminate some of her writing time in order to conduct her job search. She planned for a month of intensive searching and then a return to writing regardless of her success.

As I write, Susan is still looking for a new job. She has been searching for three months, but has not found an opportunity that meets her basic criteria. In her short-term plan, she has provided for the possibility that she might not find a new position quickly. While she searches, she devotes more energy to her other passions—cooking and nurturing her relationships with her friends. She claims her friends provide a vital life force that renews her when her job becomes too frustrating.

In the long term she has also planned for the possibility that her novels will not sell. That would certainly be disappointing, but she knows that writing will still fulfill her. She is prepared to write only for herself and sees no shame or sadness in it. She will not allow her passion to slip out of her life, but rather has planned to keep it alive in any situation. She sums up her attitude succinctly: "I'm not going to get stuck in a dream. I have to live it."

To help you understand Susan's experience in terms of planning, look over the action plan she created (Figure 6.1). Note that she changed it slightly to reflect events that have transpired in her life.

Be Proactive

Susan demonstrates an important rule you must remember in designing your action plan: be proactive. To be an executor you must view your plan as a vital, living document, an expression of your personal intensity and a harbinger of things to come. Though you can't account for every possibility and every situation, you can create your own future by envisioning it and planning for it. Susan might have dreamed for years of writing a novel, but she took the initiative to actually do it. She planned to let her passion in one hour at a time, and so ensured that every hour was better.

When you plan to let your passion in, pursuing it further should get easier. Susan's circumstances have grown more complicated since she began implementing her plan, but her commitment to working through them has remained unhindered. The plan she created has strengthened her resolve and given her the confidence to continue even when things get difficult.

As you create your action plan, remember that you are not putting up hoops to be jumped through or hurdles to be cleared. You are designing a blueprint for the life you want. Don't feel afraid to get excited about your plan, to share it with others. Through your plan, you are stating to yourself and to the world that you intend to live a passion-filled life.

Be Flexible

We have examined the need for contingencies in your plan. Implicit in contingency planning is flexibility. To survive, your plan must be flexible. It should account for different outcomes and be open to alteration based on your responses to those outcomes. This will be especially important when you encounter bumps along the road to Profit. If you assume that there is only one way for you to get where you are going, then you will be sorely disappointed when you encounter a detour.

A. Long-Term Plan (including milestones to mark my progress)

Action Step (Task/Activity)	Start/End Date(s)	Purpose and Potential Benefits for This Action
Find new job	Now–6 months	Make more time for writing/eliminate fatigue, passion drain
Résumé writing and complete second novel	6 months–2 years	Build body of work for future publishing
Attend writing workshops	Now–5 years	Develop skills; find strengths and weaknesses
Write essays and reviews (maybe short stories) for local magazines/newspapers	2 years–5 years	Build local name recognition, presence in industry
Save enough money to pay off student loans and take leave of absence	3 years–4 years	Donate 100 percent of time to writing
Make permanent transition to full-time writing	5 years–7 years	Move beyond passion-depleting work
Teach writing at university level	10 years–15 years	Share passion with others; ensure I can continually write

B. Contingency Plans

Condition	Response
Can't find new job	Begin researching new fields relevant to law *and* writing
Novels not published or unsuccessful commercially	Continue writing for pleasure; possibly make and/or change to publishing or education

Figure 6.1. Susan's Action Plan.

C. Short-Term Plan (immediate actions I can take to begin pursuing my passion)

Action Step (Task/Activity)	Start/End Date(s)	Purpose and Potential Benefits for This Action
Manage job stress by focusing on search for new job; limit hours in office to 9/day (if possible)	Today!	Change focus from negatives at present to positives at future
Research opportunities in speechwriting, nonprofit sector	Tomorrow	Find alternatives that will provide $ during transition to full-time writing
Take cooking classes	Next month	Keep this passion alive; increase general excitement level
Meet with friends once/week to get ideas and feedback on my progress	This week	Relieve pressure; build support; maintain energy level
Contact fellow alumni who have made it as writers	Next few months	Develop possible strategies for success; increase professional network
Join local writer's group, possibly union for support on professional issues, ramifications of self-employment	This month	Preparing for logistics of transition from lawyer to writer

Figure 6.1. Susan's Action Plan (cont.).

You might become frustrated and give up rather than simply change course. It is crucial for you to realize that regardless of what happens there is always another way.

The Case of May

Entrepreneurs will be the first to testify that an open mind and timely response are necessary to navigate the potholes that pop up as you follow your action plan. They face perhaps more trifling obstacles than any other group in building their livelihood around their passions. The owner of a small antique shop in the Midwest, call her May, many times has found her plans thwarted by outside forces.

Though May's hometown was thousands of miles and a world of ideas away from Asia, as a child she often spent the summer months with her grandparents in San Francisco. On these visits she would beg her grandmother to take her to Chinatown, where she spent hours in little shops, marveling at the delicate objects that adorned the shelves. Something about these things appealed to her in a way nothing else did. They preoccupied her thoughts by day and her dreams by night. Over time she came to understand it was the elegance and simplicity of their design that touched a chord in her. Though they excited her, they also brought her a sense of peace.

After graduating from college, May spent a few years in different areas of Asia, learning more about the region's history and its artisans. When she returned to the United States she decided that she would share her love of Asian design with others. Against the advice of friends and family, she opened a small Oriental antique shop in the hinterland of North America. Business was slow at first and May struggled to keep the shop afloat. Unfortunately, the town's residents seemed to favor pieces handed down from American pioneers over those shipped in from halfway around the world.

But May remained enthusiastic and vowed to find a way. If customers would not come to her, she would go to them. To build awareness within the community she held tea tastings and slide shows—in the library, in her home, and eventually in the shop. During these events she shared her knowledge and passion for things Oriental with her neighbors, and as time went by she built up a small but influential clientele. As they spread the word around the country, designers from the coast began descending on the shop, eager to snap up world-class pieces at small-town prices.

May thought she had it made. As a result of her ingenuity she had overcome a shortcoming in her plan and seemed well on her way to building a business that would stand the test of time. She opened a second store forty miles away and continued to travel to Asia twice a year to gather pieces for the shops. Then came trouble.

As May awaited a much anticipated shipment from Asia, customs officials informed her that her container would be subject to a random inspection—at her expense. Furthermore, she had to release the officials from any liability for damages incurred during the inspection or face confiscation of the container. Longshoremen opened the container on a Friday afternoon, emptying its carefully packed contents onto the dock. But the inspectors didn't finish before the end of the business day and elected to resume on Monday morning, leaving the valuable and delicate antiques exposed to the elements for more than sixty hours. Then, the hasty longshoremen crammed the hundreds of items May had spent days meticulously packing back into the container *with a forklift*! When

May finally received the container, more than a third of its contents were damaged or ruined. To a small businessperson such an event can prove catastrophic. May had no way to compensate for her loss. Even if she sold the remaining items she would not recover enough to pay for the lost items and the cost of the inspection.

To add to her problems she was forced to close the original shop because out-of-town customers now frequented her new shop, which was much closer to the airport. Her local customers remained loyal, but not numerous enough. At least she had the new shop, right? Wrong! In preparation for a major national event, the landlord of the new site elected to terminate her lease, leaving her with a container of damaged goods and no place to store them much less sell them.

May had made plans, but never in her wildest dreams had she imagined things could go like this. Resigned to defeat, May decided to pack up her bags and move to San Francisco, where at least her passion could thrive and perhaps she could find a new way to pursue it. She called her most devoted clients to say goodbye. She was not prepared for their response. They begged her to stay, assured her they would help her through her problems if only she would keep bringing them the items they too had grown to love. Within one week she had a new store and more orders than she could fill in six trips to Asia.

May learned that there is always a way if you are willing to be flexible. She admits that the new store is not in her favorite location and that she did not relish the frenzied transoceanic trips necessary to fill all the new orders. But it allowed her to continue pursuing the plan that in her heart she wanted to fulfill. Today May is thrilled to be in business and is turning a bigger profit than she ever thought possible. She has achieved the Profit she sought according to the action plan she prescribed. Though the means have changed along the way, the end has remained the same.

A Change in Passion?

The changes that affected May's action plan did not affect her passion, rather they were predicated on it. The chances she received to stay on track resulted directly from the power of her passion: it distinguished her efforts and won her the respect and devotion of her customers. But it is possible that, as you follow the plans you make, you will discover the passion you are pursuing is not really a passion but a fondness or a whim. In this case, you might decide to scrap your plan completely, or change the portions that deal specifically with that passion.

Suppose, for example, that I recently joined a computer user group with my friends. We attend meetings every other week and I come home so enthused I think I must be onto something. I enjoy working on my computer and have big ideas for improving both hardware and software. I might identify this enthusiasm as a passion and consider making a long-term move into the computer field. Because I do not have the technical knowledge I will need, I might plan to enroll in some night classes. My future plans might involve getting a degree in computer science and conducting my own consumer research.

As I begin my classes, I am immediately aware that my enthusiasm is gone. I attribute my frustration to the difficulty of the material and proceed with my coursework. After all, I still love attending the user group. As my skills improve and things become easier for me, I realize that nothing is changing.

I am not enjoying myself; that spark that I feel at the user group is simply not there.

So I begin to experiment. I drop one of the classes and spend some time teaching myself from a textbook. Maybe the teacher was getting in the way of my passion. The teacher is gone, but there is still no difference. Finally, I attend another user group that is hosting a prominent industry CEO, and much to my surprise I am similarly apathetic. What has happened to my passion? And then, at the next meeting of my own user group, it hits me. I'm not passionate about computers; I'm passionate about the discourse I have with my friends surrounding them. I'm passionate about my user group.

Needless to say, my plans for future education no longer apply. Instead of following a plan that does not reflect my passion, I need to step back, reconsider where my passions lie, and start again.

Though for most of us starting from scratch is an unlikely scenario, we need to be willing to nip and tuck our plans as we learn more about ourselves and our possibilities. For this reason, you must build flexibility into your plan. Do not marry yourself to any one detail or any one provision. Be prepared to revisit and revise. As Publilius Syrus wrote thousands of years ago, "It is a bad plan that admits no modification." Do not predicate achieving your goals on one specific course. Instead realize that the path you end up following might be one you have not yet envisioned.

Be Opportunistic

An important aspect of being flexible is opportunism. Often this term is used negatively, but I only mean that you should be willing and prepared to take advantage of any and all positive opportunities that come your way—those you plan for as well as those you do not.

A frequent comment from passioneers is, "And then this great opportunity just fell in my lap." As you begin to live with passion, more and more opportunities may begin to come to you. Often this happens because others are aware of your passion and drawn to it. It also can happen by pure chance. Pursue them regardless, even if they do not fit neatly into the plan you have prescribed, as long as they are consistent with your passion and your purpose. GO FOR IT!

Strangely, opportunities often approach cloaked as failure. For example, Bill had been fascinated by fashion since childhood. He saw people as canvases upon which designers could work their artistry, bringing bodies to life with the color, shape, and texture. He dreamed of one day creating his own line of fabrics that would have the power to transform people from their everyday selves into vestiges of glamour and elegance.

As a teenager Bill worked as an apprentice in a small tailor's shop, but he had big plans: getting a design degree and moving through the ranks of the fashion elite, eventually gaining enough acclaim to open his own design house. He did indeed graduate from a respected school and became an assistant designer with a prestigious fabric design house. The company designed and produced silks for use in men's neckwear. In his first few years, Bill worked feverishly designing entire lines for the company. He was thrilled to be enlisting his passion on a daily basis, but dismayed that his designs never seemed to make it into production. Finally, his boss told him he was not working out. The colors he chose and the patterns he created were simply too unconventional and his designs too unorthodox—just plain bad, actually, confided the boss.

Bill was crestfallen. At the time most people stayed with one employer for a lifetime, and he had planned for only two possibilities: being promoted or being passed over. Being fired, especially on the grounds that his designs were not good enough, wasn't in the plan at all. He knew that his disgrace would be common knowledge and that finding another design house job would be next to impossible. He had not the slightest clue what to do next.

As he mulled over the possibilities, Bill drew up a list of every strength he possessed and every tidbit of knowledge he had gained. Then it hit him: linings! Every piece of neckwear had to have a lining, but very few companies produced them, much less considered them worthy of serious design. He gathered his self-respect, drew up a business plan, and headed to the bank. A few days later he had a loan and was on his way to creating what eventually became a fashion empire.

Bill's failure became his opportunity. As he faced an unexpected fork in the road, he thought to himself "Why not?" As the owner of his own company, he ended up with the final word on what was good and what was not. No one would ever tell him again that his designs were less than wonderful.

The flexibility Bill displayed in adapting his plan allowed him to stick with his passion despite extreme difficulties. His ability to find opportunity in failure is common among passioneers. Most others are trained to think that, if they fail in their own eyes or the eyes of others, they are inadequate and have wasted their effort. Nothing could be further from the truth. *Failing creates opportunities.* Do not be afraid to put your pride on the line in the service of your passion. If you fail, pull yourself up by the bootstraps, reevaluate your action plan, and start again. This might seem little comfort when the sting of rejection or loss is still fresh, but if you look for doors that have opened rather than those that have closed, you might be pleasantly surprised by the results.

On the flip side of Bill's experience, consider the story of Ned, a young man without a plan when his golden opportunity arose. You should not follow Ned's example; *to give yourself the best chance at success you need to start with a plan.* But you might see opportunities can arise in any situation, especially when passion is present.

Ned grew up knowing that he would be a lawyer. His parents had always said so, and it didn't particularly bother him until he graduated from law school and realized the day of reckoning had come. He accepted a prestigious judicial clerkship in a large city. In preparation for their move, his wife Jesse, whom you may remember from an earlier chapter, began interviewing for jobs. As a writer, Jesse had worked mainly on screenplays, but her agent learned of a job writing scripts for computer games. She had a vivid imagination and was excited by the prospect of creating new worlds of monsters and overlords, so she agreed to an interview.

Ned accompanied Jesse to the interview. He was a game fanatic and his curiosity was piqued at the prospect of setting foot in the offices of a game giant. Ned had been playing video and computer games since they were invented and at age twelve was the Tron Jr. National Champion. (Tron was an arcade game popular in the early 1980s). As an adult his passion for games had become strictly recreational; he had never made a connection between his love of games and the law.

The interviewers immediately liked Jesse and the conversation soon turned to Ned, who was busy investigating in the hallway. As she described his experience and education, a strange look came over the interviewers' faces and they turned to one another. They asked Jesse if Ned could come in and chat. He did and, as Jesse tells it, "I went in for an interview, and Ned came out with a job." (Jesse got the job too, but that was no surprise.) Ned, on the verge of a distinguished law career, became not an in-house counsel or legal advisor to the game company but a producer of computer games.

On the day of Jesse's interview, Ned's passion shone like a beacon. He had no plan for it, but when opportunity arose he knew enough to take it. Without a passion-centered action plan, his ability to embrace this opportunity is unusual, and it did not come without a cost. He lost the security that was assured him as a top graduate of a top law school. He faced an unknown but foreseeably ugly reaction from his parents. He opened himself to misunderstanding and disapproval from colleagues in both fields. Ultimately, however, Ned knew that the real risk in this opportunity was not taking it. He had to follow his heart.

Since then, Ned has formulated a plan. Though he has benefited greatly from coincidence, he vows never to leave his happiness to chance again. As he learns to heed his passion, he will also learn to recognize the possibilities for its growth. Eventually he will begin to internalize much of what I have presented here and carry out his plan with little need for reminders or encouragement. He will have a constant awareness of how his decisions will affect his ability to continue living with passion. He will begin to create his own opportuni-

Passion Review

To define my actions I will . . .
- Develop an action plan for bringing passion (back) into my life
- Determine the scope, intensity, and pace with which I am prepared to begin
- Decide the specific things I can do to best develop and pursue my passion
- Develop both a long- and short-term plan
- Designate milestones for my progress
- Plan for multiple outcomes
- Prepare to be proactive, flexible, and opportunistic

ties and effect his own successes. He, like you, will become both creator and product of his action plan.

Before you move on to Step 5, review the following points.

Use Worksheet #4 to create your action plan. Be sure to include actions you can take in both the short term and the long term to help you move toward your Profit. Also prepare a contingency plan so you will be ready for possible outcomes of your actions.

Once you have created your action plan, you are ready to begin living it. In the next chapter I will show you how to implement the plan you have created here and the ways you can expect your life to improve as you do.

PASSION PLAN WORKSHEET #4

Step 4: Define Your Actions   How

A. Long-Term Plan (including milestones to mark my progress)

Action Step (Task/Activity)	Start/End Date(s)	Purpose and Potential Benefits for This Action

Organize your actions into sequential, manageable tasks/ activities. Points to consider:

- Planned schedule (target dates) for starting and completing actions
- Why do this task/activity and how do you hope to benefit?

Consider the following questions when defining your actions:

- Who else will be affected by the actions you plan to take?
- Why is this action important in pursuing your passion?
- What resources will be needed to complete the action?
- What do you have to consider not doing in order to complete an action?
- How will you know that you have been successful in carrying out each particular action?

B. Contingency Plans

Condition	Response

Focus on developing contingency plans for the most critical actions. Make the necessary people aware of these plans. Consider the following:

- What specific threats and opportunities influence the actions I plan to take?
- How will I deal with unanticipated obstacles or opportunities?
- What can be done to prevent these potential obstacles from occurring or to allow these opportunities to occur?

Passion Plan Worksheet #4 (cont.)

C. Short-Term Plan (immediate actions I can take to begin pursuing my passion)

Action Step (Task/Activity)	Start/End Date(s)	Purpose and Potential Benefits for This Action

Organize your actions into sequential, manageable tasks/activities. Points to consider:

- Planned schedule (target dates) for starting and completing actions
- Why do this task/activity and how do you hope to benefit?

Consider the following questions when defining your actions:

- Will this help me to move away from passion-depleting experiences?
- Will this inspire passion on a day-to-day level?
- Will this help me to become an executor?

CHAPTER 7

Step Five
Perform with Passion

If one advances confidently in the direction of his dreams, and endeavors to live the life which he has imagined, he will meet with a success unexpected in common hours.

HENRY DAVID THOREAU, *WALDEN*, 1854

When you live with passion, your life takes on a new quality. Under its influence you live in a heightened state, transcending the mundane, or what Thoreau termed common hours. You enter the realm of the uncommon, the domain of the supercharged. Passion kindles your senses, enhances your perceptions, and magnifies your experience. As a result you can accomplish more than you may have thought possible and meet with successes you previously only imagined. The excitement you will feel when playing out your passions is a result not only of being engaged in something you love, but also of knowing that you are living your dreams. You are making them happen.

Such euphoria might seem distant now; you are just beginning to get in touch with your passion. But if you have defined your purpose and formulated your plan, you are prepared to start a new kind of living. You are ready to become self-actualizing, or in other words, to realize your potential and live the better life you know you can achieve.

GETTING STARTED

Perhaps the most important thing you can do in preparing to implement your plan is to acknowledge that the mission on which you are embarking is an important and necessary step in your personal evolution. Integrating passion, *your* passion, into your life is not a mere technique for achieving a quick fix or instant happiness. It is an attempt to understand who you really are and to build a life around your core identity, around the things that inspire and fulfill you. You are capable of personal greatness and entitled to it, but you and only you can bring it about. By committing to your passion, you are vowing to take control of your life and to create your own self-fulfilling future.

The Passion Plan can change your life, but the level and duration of the change will depend on your commitment to this ideal. Often when start a new program we are enthusiastic. Just as often the energy falls by the wayside as the reality of the changes we must make settles in. As you begin to carry out your action plan, you probably will have mixed emotions. At times you might be uplifted by the power of your passion, and at others you might be discouraged that the world does not recognize it. I wish I could promise that your path would be free of obstacles; it will not. I wish I could assure you your changes would come effortlessly; they won't.

All the forces that worked to keep passion out of your life before will try to defeat it once you bring it back. Do not be daunted, though. You can do this! By carefully considering where you want to go and how you want to get there before leaping forward with your passion, you have prepared yourself to succeed. As you set about your plan, you are going to be creating the opportunities and the environments in which your passion can flourish and in which you can excel. You will be setting the stage for a sustained, substantive change rather than a fleeting, empty one.

FIND YOUR WAY

The plan you created in the previous chapter is the framework for putting your passion into action. Remember, however, that this framework is not rigid or static. On the contrary, it is flexible and dynamic. The milestones you set in your long-term plan and the specific actions you targeted in your short-term plan give it structure; the experiences you build as you live your plan give it context and meaning. As you begin to carry out your action plan, the ways you can best reach your Profit will become more evident. An important aspect of performing with passion is looking for options as you go and finding those that best fit you and your circumstances. To this end, do three things as you begin to move toward your goals: investigate, communicate, and assess. Each will help you define your options and determine which is best suited to your nature and your plan.

Investigate

"Don't reinvent the wheel," people say. This is true when carrying out your action plan. There are valuable lessons to be learned from the experiences of others. Whatever goal you set, whatever change you seek has been done before. Certainly your pursuit is unique, as will be your accomplishment, but by investigating the ways others have succeeded (and failed) you can save a lot of time, energy, and frustration.

Many people, for example, want to leave the corporate world and work for themselves. If self-employment is one of your goals, first learn how others have made the transition. Research leaders in your field and in your community who have achieved what you want to achieve. Contact them, ask their advice, and consider taking it. If they have learned the ins and outs of self-promotion, the intricacies of local business regulations, or the practices that win customer trust, use their knowledge to your benefit. More important, if they share your passion for your field, ask them how they have utilized it to move forward with their business.

Your investigation need not be limited to personal interviews. Read magazines, newspapers, and journals. Contact organizations and institutions related to your profession. Do research in libraries and on the Internet. Be aggressive in your search for information; the rewards will be well worth the effort. Using your newly gained insight, you will be better prepared to avoid obstacles and be primed to put your passion into play wisely and effectively.

Communicate

In conducting your research, you may gain not only knowledge but relationships with people who can become both friends and mentors. Discuss your options with people whose personal or professional opinions you value. Once you choose the steps you will take, run them by these confidants and solicit their opinions. If they know you well and sense your passion, their insight can be invaluable. One of them might even serve as a personal coach—someone you can turn to regularly for instruction and feedback as you begin to live your passion. Though ultimately change must come from within, coaches can provide external incentives for moving forward. Based on their experience and expertise, they can help you build the skill, knowledge, motivation, and confidence you need to succeed. This can be especially important in the early stages of your action plan when you are most vulnerable and most likely to wane in your commitment.

Assess

After you have investigated methods and communicated your ideas to others, evaluate what you have learned and decide how you can best approach reaching your milestones. Though others can add fresh perspectives and provide insights, only you can determine what steps will work best for you. This does not mean you should take the easiest road; the best path might be the one that requires you to push yourself harder or in new ways. Your decision should be based on an understanding of your strengths and weaknesses and how they will have an impact on your future success.

To illustrate, let's say you are an organized, efficient self-starter and want to start your own business. Your best alternative might be setting up shop at home and working alone. If, however, you feed on the energy of others and cringe at the thought of recordkeeping and self-administration, you might consider finding a partner or joining with others who

Passion Review

As you start performing with passion, do the following:

- *Investigate:* find out what has worked for others in the past
- *Communicate:* talk to others who can advise and encourage you
- *Assess:* evaluate your options and choose those best suited to you and your situation

complement your strengths and compensate for your weaknesses. Admitting your shortcomings in no way diminishes the power of your passion, nor does it mean you will not work to overcome them. Similarly, embracing your strengths does not mean you will not work at developing other abilities. Doing so simply allows you to predicate your success on the qualities you possess as opposed to those you lack.

CREATE YOUR ENVIRONMENT

As you begin to implement your action plan, you will have good days and bad days. Sometimes you can barely contain your excitement for your new life or your relief at moving away from the old one. Other days you question the worth of your efforts. Even the strongest of passioneers is subject to temporary bouts of discouragement. To minimize them and to maximize the flow of passion in your life, take steps to create an environment where your passion can thrive.

To do this, consider what in your environment—where you live and work, the people around you—that feed your passion or stifles it. For centuries Eastern civilizations have recognized that people possess an underlying energy that can be either enhanced or impaired by their surroundings. Factors such as space, lighting, and design all affect the quality of your life by eliciting your basic energy or killing it. If there is harmony in your surroundings, so will there by harmony in your life. If there is discord, difficulties could result, even sickness. A rapidly growing modern-day industry has evolved from the traditional art of Feng Shui, revolving around the design of spaces that are conducive to personal happiness and success.

Whether you believe in a mystical life force or simply want to get more done, you can make changes in your physical environment to help elicit and feed your passion. The suggestions that follow may seem obvious, but it is surprising how few of us ever take the simple steps to optimize our surroundings.

Surround Yourself with Reminders of Your Passion

You should honor your passion. It a vital part of you, so acknowledge it in the places you spend time. We do this instinctively as children. Think back to the bedroom of your adolescent years. How many posters of rock groups or supermodels or mythical animals did you plaster on your walls? How many tokens of your achievements—trophies, ribbons, certificates—filled the space? If something bored or offended you, chances are you got rid of it. If it moved you or meant something special, you assigned it a spot of reverence.

Somehow as we grow older we forget how important these reminders can be. Look around your home or office and consider how much of what you see really reflects who you are. Are most of the furnishings and accessories things you chose or things that were given to you by a boss or spouse or parent? Are you hanging onto things you don't like because you don't want the expense of replacing them or are too lazy to get rid of them? Are you afraid to display items that are special to you for fear others will disapprove?

The bottom line is you will perform better and feel more inspired if you are reminded of your passion through visual cues. If you love books and they inspire you to think, write, or dream, stock your home with bookshelves instead of filling boxes in the basement with last month's novels. If you dream of one day becoming an aviator, hang model planes from the ceiling or pictures of Lindbergh and Earhart on the walls. If you want to win an award, above your desk post articles about it or a list of reasons for wanting it. As simple and frivolous as these examples may sound, they work. It is hard to forget or ignore what you're seeking if it's staring you in the face. Similarly, it is easy to remember your feelings and fuel them further when you are inspired by what you see.

Create Physical Conditions Conducive to Progress

Light fixtures and chairs can interfere with personal development. Not that certain light bulbs or upholstery emit negative energy, but they can impede your progress if they make you uncomfortable. If your work centers around a desk, then that desk should accommodate your basic needs. If you have to strain your eyes due to poor lighting, hunch your back because of insufficient lumbar support, or constantly fiddle with temperature controls or window blinds, it is harder to sustain your energy. Similarly, if the dull gray walls of your office leave you feeling sad or the chartreuse shade in the bathroom makes you nauseated, it's going to be hard for your passion to break through.

I used to laugh when a friend told me that the fluorescent lights above her desk at work were literally sucking the life out of her. She felt her skin was turning sallow and her mood depressed. She tried a different bulb, soft pink as opposed to bright white, but still found it hard to function. Eventually she found that she was much happier and able to get much more done if she turned out the overhead lights and worked by the warm yellow light of a desk lamp she brought from home. Whether there is any physiological or chemical validity to her theory is irrelevant. What is relevant is that her work and her passion were suffering, and when she changed her environment the situation improved.

Lest you think only women are so sensitive, a man I know, an executive in a large computer company, often brings his work home and stays up into the wee hours of the morning writing letters, responding to e-mail, and preparing presentations. Even with all his years of experience and expertise, he cannot work effectively during those hours unless music is playing. He bought a 200-CD changer so that at the push of a button he could have hours of uninterrupted listening. Ironically, his wife, who also hammers away on her laptop late into the night, cannot work with music, so they find themselves in separate ends of the house.

Live in a Place That Inspires You

In the larger sense, you can choose the place you live based on these same responses. I do not mean your house or apartment, although this certainly applies. I mean the country, state, or city you call home. A doctor I know, upon finishing medical school, chose to perform his residency in Colorado strictly to be near the mountains. He was an avid, though not particularly talented, skier and had spent brief periods during breaks and vacations working at a ski resort. Something about the mountains kindled a fire in him and he knew his life would be more intense and more fulfilling if he lived near them. After completing his residency, he and his wife built their dream home high in the mountains outside Denver. His commute time to work was over ninety minutes, but he was happy to make the drive each day. He felt more alive, more inspired, more energized than ever before. His wife, however, is more of a beach person. But, she said, "We have an unwritten rule that every vacation we take is to the beach. There is no discussion. He gets the mountains throughout the year, and I get the beach on holidays."

I am not suggesting that everyone should pick up and move to the nearest natural wonder that awes them. But weigh your gut response to various settings before deciding where to live and work, if you can. A city that fills you with energy seems an obvious choice over a town that fills you with dread. Why, after all, live in a place that you dislike? Unless the law or your mother is keeping you there against your will, you do have options. If you love the countryside and have always dreamed of living the simple life, try spending some time in more rural environs. If you feel revitalized by the hustle and bustle of the city, take an apartment down-town for a period. Do whatever you can, within the realm of your personal possibilities, to live in a place that will inspire and feed your passion.

Spend Time with People Who Feed Your Passion

There is an old saying, "You can choose your friends, but you can't choose your family." True, but we need to give more thought to the quality of our relationships with family members and the ways we choose not only our friends but also our coworkers and associates. Other people are one of our most valuable resources in invoking our passion. They cannot force us to feel it, but they can draw it out or discourage it.

So examine the relationships in your life and determine which are enabling and which are stultifying. Build friend-ships and associations with people who share and support your goals. The people you spend time with should challenge you to become better, rather than engaging you at a lower level. Parents want this for their children and work actively to eliminate "bad influences" from their lives. Often, however, they do not set such a high standard for themselves.

The influence others bring to bear on us is not merely a function of whether they do drugs, listen to loud music, or run with the wrong crowd. Sometimes we are attracted to people irrespective of their lifestyle choices, for reasons we do not understand. You probably have had a friend, teacher, or boss who you wanted desperately to impress. Unless your desire stemmed from physical attraction, this person somehow brought out something higher in you, something more than you normally were prepared to give. You struggled to speak more authoritatively, to act more decisively, to be the person you knew you could be.

By choosing to spend time with people who spark this desire, who inspire you to try harder and think more clearly, you actively engage and nurture your passion on a daily basis. Even though you cannot choose your parents or children, you can choose how you interact with them. Seek to cultivate relationships with them that develop your passion in similar ways. Share your passion with family members and seek to understand theirs. Avoid situations and topics that lead time and time again to disagreements and bad feelings. Look for new experiences to share and new ways of communicating about them. If you are dedicated to bringing these relationships to a higher level and to integrating passion into them, you will succeed.

Refine Your Routines

Part of the environment you create for yourself is determined by the routines you set. Whether we like it or not, we all have habits. Even the most spontaneous person often wakes up or goes to sleep in the same way from day to day. Your morning routine might include a shower, a cup of coffee, and a newspaper. Mine might entail a danish, a morning news program, and a jog around the block. Though you might not be aware of it, your routine could affect your ability to work passion into your life. Your daily rituals might actually squelch your energy and prevent your passion from emerging. By changing your routines you might find that things that once seemed difficult become easy.

Consider a writer I know who, for years, woke up every morning and set straight to writing. Though he always struggled during the morning hours, he felt this was necessary to meet the daily quota he had set for himself. One morning a deliveryman interrupted him; he felt he had lost his momentum so he sat down for a big breakfast and a leisurely reading of his favorite magazine. When he returned to writing later, he found the words came more easily. The next morning he tried it again—eat, read, then work—and experienced similar results. From that moment on his routine had officially changed. One minor alteration in his schedule improved the quality and quantity of his work as well as his mood throughout the day.

Experiment with the order and timing of your activities. You might be surprised at the difference it makes. Also, try the unexpected. Introduce new practices or revert to ones that

 Passion Review

To maximize the flow of passion in your life, take the following steps to create an environment where your passion can thrive:

- Surround yourself with reminders of your passion
- Create the physical conditions most conducive to your progress
- Live in a place that inspires you
- Spend time with people who feed your passion
- Refine your routines

worked in the past. The bottom line is to work and play in ways that leave you receptive to your passion or actually inspire it.

LET YOURSELF GO

Clear your head for a moment of all the concerns you might have about implementing your action plan. You have plenty to think about, but do not be overwhelmed with the details. You have a plan and you are prepared to act on it. Soon the actions you begin to take will become almost natural. Even if you face resistance, passion will become second nature to you. The most important thing you can do now is to let yourself go, to begin to experience your passion and to benefit from it.

Consider the reasons you are doing this. Why do you want passion to be a part of your life? To live a great life, to be all you can, to reach your full potential. In discussing our chronic failure to reach our potential, the noted psychologist William James (1977 [1902]) wrote, "Stating the thing broadly, the human individual thus lives usually far within his limits; he possesses powers of various sorts which he habitually fails to use. He energizes below his *maximum,* and behaves below his *optimum.*" A part of us knows when we are not doing the most or best we can. James observed:

> Every one is familiar with the phenomenon of feeling more or less alive on different days. Every one knows on any given day that there are energies slumbering in him which the incitements of that day do not call forth, but which he might display if these were greater. Most of us feel as if a sort of

cloud weighed upon us, keeping us below our highest notch of clearness in discernment, sureness in reasoning, or firmness in deciding. Compared with what we ought to be, we are only half awake. Our fires are damped, our drafts are checked.

What powerful imagery! The key to better living, as James saw it, is finding ways to incite this energy. I concur. This is exactly what you are doing by integrating passion into your life. Your passions are the things that rustle your soul to consciousness and help you harness your underlying energies.

PEAK EXPERIENCE

As mentioned previously, doubtless you have had moments where you have felt the energy coursing through your veins and sensed your innate potential. In the world of psychology, these moments are known as *peak experiences*. Abraham Maslow, father of the school of thought known as humanistic psychology, described such occurrences as moments of self-actualization. They are, he claimed,

> episode[s] . . . in which the powers of the person come together in a particularly efficient and intensely enjoyable way, and in which he is more integrated and less split, more open for experience, more idiosyncratic, more perfectly expressive or spontaneous, or fully functioning, more creative, more humorous, more ego-transcending, more independent of his lower needs, etc. He becomes in these episodes more truly himself, more perfectly actualizing his

potentialities, closer to the core of his Being, more fully human [1968].

Certainly when we experience these moments we do not expend our energy pondering them. Rather we become caught up in them, completely absorbed in their power.

During peak experiences we lose our sense of time. We are usually surprised afterward that so many minutes or hours have passed. We perform effortlessly, as if we are on autopilot. Something seems to take over and we are more efficient, more capable than our abilities would normally suggest. We also feel at once more alive and more powerful. Our senses are heightened and we tingle with an energy we cannot explain. We feel invincible, in complete control of the task at hand.

Athletes often describe their episodes of peak performance with phrases such as "in the zone" and "on fire." Artists, musicians, and writers provide similar accounts of their creative powers surging, enabling them to create their greatest works with little perceived effort. Public speakers stand before crowds of thousands and feel overcome by the power of the message they seek to deliver. They characterize their orations as coming from a source other than themselves. Words flash into their minds and pass through their lips as quickly and effortlessly as they arrive. Bond traders, advertising executives, cashiers, and race-car drivers all are subject to peak experiences. With a challenge to meet, they can rise to new levels and encounter great joy in doing so.

Consider your own peak experiences. Can you remember them? Can you recall how you felt and what you accomplished under their influence? It should not be difficult; usually memories of peak experiences are vivid and their impact lasting. Imagine now how your life would be if you could control when and where you had peak experiences. What could you do or be if they were the norm and not the exception?

The reason for identifying and calling on your passions is so your life can become an extended peak experience, a sustained encounter in self-actualization. When you do this, you enter what I call the passion zone. Passioneers live in the passion zone; they are both enthusiastic and satisfied with their lives. These feelings are an outgrowth of the empowerment and initiative that result from performing at their peak. The advantage passioneers hold is that they build their lives around the things that will call up this potential rather than defeat it.

Let's consider how this works. There seem to be a number of factors critical to triggering peak experiences. The first is that you are engaged in something that is important to you. This is why, as you recall your past experiences, they probably focus around people or activities about which you care deeply. You are far more likely to enter a heightened state on the golf course or in the boardroom if you want to be there in the first place.

The second factor is that you are trying to accomplish a specific goal or reward. An athlete might seek to win a race or set a record. An artist might hope to gain recognition or create a new style of painting. An entrepreneur might aspire to win customers or persuade investors. Whatever the challenge, there must be some standard by which you can gauge your ultimate performance. Even if you are your only audience and your standard is exceeding your personal expectations, you must have some means of recognizing the results of your experience.

The third factor is focus. Peak experiences are predicated on concentration. Your energies and faculties must be centered on the activity at hand if you are to enter your zone. If you are distracted or troubled, you will not be able to achieve your peak until you eliminate these extraneous concerns from your field of thought. Psychologist Mihalyi Csikszentmihalyi goes so far as to assert that we can perform at our peak, or flow, in any given activity if we only apply sufficient concentration. Although there may be some truth in this, most of us find it difficult to devote ourselves so wholeheartedly to things we do not like or truly care about.

This is why passion is so critical. We can wait for peak experiences to happen randomly, or we can actively seek them by bringing passion into our lives. Our passions are the key to bringing out our best, to triggering peak experiences, and to realizing our full potential. As you carry out your action plan, you will see increased opportunities to extend yourself and enlist your passions. You will create the situations in which

 Passion Review

To trigger peak experiences, I should . . .

- Engage in activities that are important to me
- Have specific goals I am trying to accomplish
- Focus exclusively on the activity at hand

your abilities will shine and your possibilities will expand. With patience, effort, and desire you will begin consistently performing at your peak.

PERFORMING IN PARALLEL

I mentioned earlier that in the throes of peak experience we feel invincible. As you transform your life from passion-lacking to passion-filled, you will feel more powerful. You will sense that you are capable of more than you imagined. Part of this increased awareness will be a recognition that you can work toward multiple goals or Profit areas simultaneously.

Traditionally we have been taught that to excel in any one area we must give it our undivided attention. I disagree. I strongly believe that as long as we are passionate about the things we are pursuing we can pursue them in tandem without sacrificing our progress in any one area. Not only that, our varied accomplishments can work together to serve our greater goals. I call this performing in parallel.

A client from Saudi Arabia recently attended a training seminar at my corporate headquarters. When the seminar facilitator introduced us, he acted confused. He said he expected me to be much older and somehow more distinguished looking. I took this as a compliment, because his surprise reflected my accomplishments. I have built my business based on the achievements of twenty-five years rather than the forty or fifty people often expect. The reason I have done so much in so little time is my commitment to performing in parallel.

The decade or so after I graduated from college was perhaps the most critical for me in terms of laying the foundations for the life I desired. I knew that any business I would build in the future relied on the credentials and experiences I built in the present. I decided that graduate school, work experience, and involvement in professional organizations were all necessary components of my future success, and I pursued them all aggressively. At one point I was a full-time student in a doctoral program, a full-time employee of a large corporation, a part-time lecturer at a local university, and the president of a local chapter of a professional society. You might wonder how I could manage to fit in so much in so little time, but you would be amazed what careful planning and time management can produce. More important, I did not feel overwhelmed by the diversity of my involvements, but rather fueled by it. I knew that I was working toward something important, toward the life I wanted.

Certainly it is possible to spread yourself too thin. Had I been married or had children, I could not have immersed myself in my academic and professional pursuits so deeply. Likewise if I had wanted to pursue my bowling career at a higher level, I would have been forced to scale back my other activities. But given the state of my life at the time, I had no reason not to chase down my dreams on a full-time basis by going after each and every accomplishment I felt important. My passion provided all the energy I needed to keep me going.

If your action plan provides for a slightly less frenetic pace than mine did, you can still accomplish many things at once. One of the most inspiring women I know has managed to expand her range of ability and achievement by implementing her plan in parallel mode. At the age of twenty-six,

Janice found herself living a life she never imagined. She had a husband, three children, and no college degree. A brilliant writer and a talented student, Janice had always planned on getting a doctorate, although in what field she was not sure. As her life unfolded, however, she began to feel this was no longer possible. She married at twenty-one, and much to her shock and dismay got pregnant three times despite her fervent attempts to prevent it.

Janice was quickly forced out of the role of student and into the roles of mother and breadwinner. Because her husband was also young and just entering the workforce, they knew a double income was a necessity. Perhaps hearkening to her passion for education, Janice found a job at a university as an administrative assistant in a research laboratory. She immediately excelled and within two years was running the lab. She had turned a once floundering financial operation into a profitable venture. As a result, she found herself making more money than she would have had she received her degree and worked in another field.

As the years passed, Janice gained confidence as an administrator but lost faith in her promise as a student. She resigned herself to her chance profession and the economic gains it brought. But one day something changed. A colleague began urging her to reenroll at the university. He recognized her promise and the silent frustration she suffered at her job. She could attend part time and for half tuition, so why not indulge herself a little? Doubting herself every step of the way, Janice took her entrance exams and completed her application.

The university recognized the same potential in Janice that her friend did and rewarded her with both admission and encouragement. Once she began her coursework, her fears quickly abated. Her passion for writing and study reignited and she knew she had to make a change. Together she and her husband developed a plan by which she could gradually make the transition from full-time employee to full-time student. His income was increasing steadily from year to year, and though it would take years for him to earn alone what they had earned together, they felt the financial sacrifice was well worth the happiness it would bring her.

Today Janice is one semester away from completing her degree. Her plans for the future include a doctorate and a career as either a writer or professor. She has already won numerous writing awards and is respected as a scholar of great promise.

Janice's experience with performing in parallel is quite different from my own. I worked rapidly; her pace was less extreme. I focused mainly on myself; she focused on her family as well. Janice worked diligently as a student, a mother, a wife, and a professional, none to the detriment of the other. She says her ability to do so much so well arose from the passion she brought back into play by returning to school. She had always loved and enjoyed her family, but she found she was more alive, more capable, more invigorated when studying was present in her life. By bringing her passion back in, she was empowered to perform at her peak.

LETTING PASSION INFORM YOUR DECISIONS

Today when Janice is faced with a choice, she forms her decision in a completely different way than she did before. She does not consider whether her choices are in keeping with the expectations of the world or concerns she does not share, but whether they will feed her passion and enable her to keep it alive and thriving. She recognizes that if she acts in defiance of her passion, she can lose it just as easily as she found it.

Part of carrying out your action plan is making decisions in circumstances both expected and unexpected. You might plan how to respond if you get your dream job or if you don't, but you might not plan what to do if you are offered a completely different job. You also might not consider what you would do if the responses you have taken for granted don't materialize. Plenty of people have landed a dream job only to realize it is not what they expected. In such a case, look to your heart for answers.

A case in point is the famous artist mentioned in Chapter One. Though he always knew he had to draw, he did not feel a necessity to be a professional artist. In fact, after graduating from graduate school he opted to be an art teacher, because teaching was also a passion for him. As he said, "I love to help people understand things they don't already understand. I love to expose them to new ideas and to open them to new worlds. When that moment of learning comes, it's like turning the lights on. You can see it in their eyes."

After five years of teaching junior high art, he knew he couldn't keep doing it. While his passion for teaching was strong, his passion for art was even stronger. He had been painting in his spare time but found his energy for painting diminishing as a result of his teaching. His initial enthusiasm had been sapped by the financial constraints and bureaucracy of the school system. When he asked himself, "How am I going to make my mark on history?" he knew teaching was not the way. He knew he had to make a change.

He took a leave of absence, but secretly knew he would never return. He did not know what direction he was headed because he had never really considered life outside teaching. To pay the bills he taught part-time at a junior college, but he was so uncomfortable in this role he developed ulcers. In the meantime he focused on his painting, not as a means of generating income but as an expression of his passion. Before he painted people, wildlife, and foliage because he felt it was what potential buyers wanted. Despite his great skill at that, he had not found a unique voice for his art. His trees looked much the same as the next artist's.

His breakthrough came when he gave into his "guilty pleasures" and painted what truly excited him—the mythological characters and creatures that lurked in his imagination. Today his art falls into the category of fantasy, depicting gnomes, hunchbacks, flying fish, and angels. He now has a tremendous following, but in the early days he was sure few would care for his whimsy. He painted anyway, hoping only to indulge his passion and sell enough paintings to keep his studio stocked with paints, brushes, and canvases.

Despite the potential hazard to the family's financial condition, he and his wife agreed he could not return to teaching. The itch inside him was one teaching simply could not scratch. Remarkably, he received a call from a magazine that was familiar with his graduate work and a request to join the staff as an illustrator. He jumped at the chance, viewing it as opportunity to make more money in an environment that would feed rather than drain his passion.

Though he was getting paid to create more standard images than those he loved, this did not worry him. He continued to indulge his passion for fantasy art in his free time.

He displayed some of his personal work at weekend shows and even sold a few paintings along the way. After three years at the magazine, his alma mater, located only forty miles away, contacted him regarding a professor position. He was thrilled. It was the opportunity he had always dreamed of. As a professor of art he would have a secure career centered on art that also gave him lots of "wiggle room" for pursuing his own art. He could teach free of the constraints of the junior high and replete with the perquisites of the university—significant resources, notable colleagues, and eager students.

When he began his tenure as professor, he did not imagine what awaited him. When classes were in session, he got a rush from teaching that carried over into his evening painting. During summers and vacations he worked, or as he likes to say, played at his art and eventually developed a signature style that distinguished him from his counterparts. As his work gained a greater audience through university and fantasy shows, a national art workshop asked him about producing and promoting his work for commercial release.

What had begun as a guilty pleasure soon became a second career. In the ensuing years, his income from his art has far exceeded his income from teaching. In fact, many are surprised that he sticks with teaching after gaining such high acclaim and financial reward in the art world. The reason is the same reason he became a successful artist: he remains true to his passion. Art has never been about money for him. It is a nice benefit, but to walk away from teaching, which has been a source of energy, comfort, and enthusiasm and has fueled his passion for painting, would be an insult to the passion that enabled his success.

As you follow your plan and make decisions of your own, you cannot expect the world to fall at your feet, but you can expect benefits at this time unforeseen. This artist told me of friends who, though equally passionate about their art, have achieved little or no commercial success. He believes some lack the necessary talent, and others have not found the inspiration that would make them unique. Some who are inspired paint subjects he collectively refers to as "camel bottoms," or things that are of little interest to the general public. In each case he can think of, however, those who are truly pursuing their art out of passion are doing so without regret. The reason may be, as he suggests, that they simply "can't bear not to do it" and by doing what they must, they are succeeding.

EVALUATING YOUR PROGRESS

After kicking off your action plan, you should begin to reap the rewards of your efforts almost immediately. You will not achieve all your goals in one day or week or month, but you will find yourself happier in your daily activities, optimistic about the future, and, hopefully, encountering more than a few peak experiences. Though things might be tough if you are making particularly difficult changes or bucking up against deep-seeded fears, you should feel something within you responding. If you are not, if nothing is changing, you will need to reevaluate your plan and perhaps more importantly your passions. No matter what you encounter along the way, your passion will bring you to new heights. It will provide you a glimpse into what you can become and a means of achieving it.

As you perform with passion, your life will change. You must be sure, however, that you do not take these changes for

Passion Review

To perform with passion I will . . .

- Begin to make the changes I outlined in my action plan
- Work to surround myself with people and places that feed my passion
- Engage in activities and routines that strengthen my passion
- Open myself to peak experiences
- Pursue many passions or aspects of my passion simultaneously (perform in parallel)
- Make sure passion informs all of my decisions

granted. You must commit to maintaining them. To help you do this, remember the following points.

To help you begin to perform with passion, complete Worksheet #5. Be sure to list the different ways you can investigate, communicate, and assess your action plan as you begin to follow it. Take a few moments to consider as well your personal performance boosters and busters, and target specific changes you can make to support yourself in carrying out your plan.

Once you have begun to perform with passion, you will be prepared to move on to Steps Six and Seven, which involve spreading your passion and persisting in your plan. Neither precedes the other in importance or necessity, because both are critical to ensuring the future success of your efforts. As you read further, remember that you can do this. If you have made it this far, you are already well on your way to reaching your Profit.

PASSION PLAN WORKSHEET #5

Step 5: Perform with Passion	How
A. Ways I Can Investigate My Action Plans:	Investigate ways that others have succeeded (and failed) in pursuing their own passion. Consider the following: • Are my actions equally important? • Have I researched others who have succeeded in living the passion I am pursuing? What lessons-learned did they have? • What organizations or associations exist that relate to my passion? What do they have to share that can help me?
B. Ways I Can Communicate: *My Action Plans*	Determine who you should communicate with regarding your actions and solicit their opinions. Although feedback is always valuable, remember that you are ultimately responsible for your actions and choices. Consider the following: • Have I communicated with trusted confidants about my actions?

Passion Plan Worksheet #5 (cont.)

B. Ways I Can Communicate (cont.):

My Action Plans (cont.)

- Have I identified a potential coach who can give me honest feedback as I pursue my passion?
- Am I clear on the message(s) I want to communicate to those around me who might be affected?

C. Ways I Can Assess My Action Plans:

Evaluate what you've learned from investigating and communicating your action plans. Make appropriate refinements, but avoid taking the easy path. Consider the following:

- What changes do I need to make to the actions I have planned?
- Have I discovered an action I need to take that I overlooked?
- Do I need to reprioritize the actions I have planned?

Passion Plan Worksheet #5 (cont.)

D. The Environment I Need to Create Around Me:	Identify the changes you need to make to your physical environment to help elicit and feed your passion. Consider the following: • Have I surrounded myself with reminders of my passion? • Are the physical conditions around me conducive to progress? • Do I live in a place that inspires me? • Am I spending time with people who feed my passion? • What routines and/or habits do I need to refine?
E. My Personal Performance Boosters Include:	List the activities, people, experiences, and behaviors that can help nurture your passion and keep you focused on pursuing your action plan. Consider the following: • What activities help me experience and live my passion? • Which people fuel my passion most?

Passion Plan Worksheet #5 (cont.)

E. My Personal Performance Boosters Include (cont.):	• Are there experiences I need to have that I have not pursued? • Do I display behaviors that support the pursuit of my passion?
F. My Personal Performance Busters Include:	List the activities, people, experiences, and behaviors that can prevent you from feeding your passion and pursuing your action plan. Consider the following: • What activities do I participate in that keep me from living my passion? • Which people in my life serve as distractions to pursuing my passion? • Are there experiences I've had that have drained me of my passion? • Do I display behaviors that don't support the pursuit of my passion?

CHAPTER 8

Step Six
Spread Your Excitement

I think that, as life is action and passion, it is required of a man that he should share the passion and action of his time at peril of being judged not to have lived.

OLIVER WENDELL HOLMES JR.

Not long ago I was doing research and came across an article giving advice to new college graduates seeking jobs. According to the article, the single most important factor in interviewing is not knowledge, experience, or poise. It is passion. The author argued that employers are more easily persuaded by candidates who show enthusiasm for the job they are seeking. They are more likely to offer a job to such people than to someone with better credentials but less enthusiasm. Passion, it seems, is contagious. When we exhibit it, others—interviewers, coworkers, and family members—are persuaded to invest in us. They give us opportunities they otherwise might not; they believe in our capabilities; they support our endeavors. In a nutshell, they help us to carry out our Passion Plan.

There are many reasons you should actively share your passion. Keeping it to yourself will only weaken your resolve and deny you invaluable resources—namely the time and energy of others. If you are pursuing your passion in a professional setting, the importance of others is readily apparent. You need your bosses to challenge you to perform and recognize your achievements once you do. You need your employees to work with you rather than against you. You need your clients or customers to trust you and desire your products or services.

If you play out your passion privately, the ways others affect you might not be as obvious. Let's say you are training for a marathon. Think how much easier your road to success would become if your spouse and children supported you in your hopes. They might encourage you when you doubt yourself, perform some of your household duties so you have more free time, research training methods, and cheer you on when you compete. If you do not have a family, the same could be true of friends and colleagues.

Regardless of the strength of your passion, you will never be completely self-sufficient. You need support, whether emotional, financial, or professional. Sometimes, under the pretense of being strong or independent, we lose sight of how important others are to us. As passioneers, we must recognize that those around us are conduits for our passion. It can flow through them and back to us. They can carry it to others we do not reach and return it in the form of shared excitement. They can provide feedback that energizes, perform tasks that strengthen, and contribute ideas and resources that improve.

CREATE A PERCEPTION

Consider for a moment the image you project. Do you share your emotions and the things that are important to you, or do you keep your feelings hidden? Do you make yourself accessible on an emotional level when others need help, or seek such help yourself when in need? Can those around you sense your energy? Are they eager to spend time with you or be involved in your activities?

Your answers might vary depending on how you have integrated passion into your life. In those areas where passion is present, chances are it shows. Others will sense your vitality and your commitment and be drawn to it. They will seek your company, solicit your advice, and try to please you. You will exude the confidence and satisfaction of one who is self-aware and self-directed, qualities that so many lack.

By living with passion, you create a perception in the minds of others as someone worthy of their commitment. This is an especially important asset when you are in a leadership role. If those you lead detect a lack of enthusiasm or wavering conviction in you, they might lose their willingness to follow you. I read recently of an NFL quarterback who went to his coach and told him that he (the quarterback) was having just such a problem. He was experiencing what I call a passion lag. As he told the coach, his heart was no longer in the game. He could have buried his problem and waited for the coach to figure it out based on his declining performance; instead he went to him as a preventive measure in the hope of getting support in revitalizing his passion. Instead of offering help, the coach handed him his pink slip. He had no place on the team for a dispassionate leader.

The coach's behavior was extreme, and there may have been more to the story than reported. Regardless of the details, however, the football community recognized the danger in a player who had lost his initiative. If a professional athlete loses his passion, he loses the fire that sparks performance, that commands the respect of coaches and other players, and that attracts fans and television audiences. He becomes a liability rather than an asset. Think about it. How have your favorite players reached their esteemed position in your heart? Would they remain your favorites if they were not excited about what they were doing? Could you tell if their hearts were no longer in the game?

The same is true of others in the public eye. Our perception of actors and politicians are predicated on the passion we detect in them. A political leader can encounter scandal after scandal and we will stand by her if we sense a burning dedication to her office and her electorate. Though passion cannot be equated with sincerity, we can detect an underlying devotion and enthusiasm in her defenses and are willing to overlook her transgressions. We are, however, unforgiving if an actor delivers a performance that is devoid of passion. This is an interesting commentary on the nature of passion, because the actor's passion is not manifested simply as heightened emotion. Although it can allow him to deliver moving performances of highly emotional characters, it enables him to be equally powerful in emotionless roles. No matter the character, something inside us connects with the performance and can detect the fervor with which the actor approaches it. If we are not convinced, we grow disillusioned and skeptical.

As you grow more familiar and more comfortable with your passion, do not be afraid to openly exhibit it to others.

They will sense your intensity and sincerity and reward you for it. A kindergarten teacher taught me just how great a difference this can make. Isabel was beginning her first year of teaching at a school where the parents were known to be the teachers' greatest supporters but also their greatest critics. She knew that by replacing one of the school's most beloved senior teachers her every move would be subject to scrutiny. She was not afraid of losing her job, as other neophytes had in the past, but of winning the support of her students and the greater school community.

The children's class assignments were posted at the school the evening before classes began, and by the next morning the principal had been put on notice by one parent that she did not want her son in Isabel's classroom. She made this protest based on nothing more than Isabel's rookie status. The principal convinced her to give Isabel a chance and agreed to change her son's assignment if she was not pleased by the end of the week. When Friday arrived, you could not have paid this mother to leave Isabel's side. She was won over.

What Isabel brought to the classroom, and what both parents and students alike could not resist, was passion. She had entered the field of education because she loved children and, more important, because she loved helping them learn. She selected the primary grades as her specialty because she saw these early years as a unique window for opening children's eyes to the wonders and possibilities of the world. The classroom she had created over the summer was an expression of her enthusiasm; it was a bright, engaging space designed not to please her but to stimulate the children. Everything she did, from patiently working one-on-one with each child to comforting the parents who were suffering from their own separation anxiety, spoke to her overwhelming desire to be exactly where she was.

Of the many parents who eagerly volunteered to participate in the classroom, one recalls the exact moment she became Isabel's most ardent supporter: "I was helping the children color and label paper dragons when Isabel pulled me aside. She looked earnest and excited at the same time. She told me that Jeremy had read his first word that morning. To hear her tell it you would have thought it was one of the world's greatest miracles. She was genuinely thrilled that she had witnessed such an important event in his little life. As she gushed with enthusiasm I could see she was tearing up, proud of his achievement and hers as well. After she was done I found myself moved to tears as well. Imagine that . . . over an everyday kindergarten occurrence."

I could tell you that Isabel had discovered the key to classroom management and parent-teacher bonding, but I would be belying the matter. What she exhibited was no technique or strategy arrived upon after careful judgment and experimentation; it was what came naturally to her. Her passion for teaching the children spoke for itself. It convinced the parents to support her and the children to follow her. In their eyes, she was not just caring and competent; she was exceptional, as worthy of praise and respect as the most seasoned of her colleagues.

ACCOMPLISH YOUR OBJECTIVES

As passion strengthens your credibility, you will find it easier to accomplish your objectives. Isabel found this to be true in a number of ways. Parents practically bent over backward to contribute their time and resources to ensure the classroom ran smoothly. The school administration aided her in speeding through her probationary status, doing everything it could to ensure her tenure. The children inspired her with smiles and gratitude, and many were reluctant to leave her side even when school had ended.

When I decided to start my own business after a decade of working for someone else, I relied on my passion to rouse the support of those who could help make my dreams a reality. I had been working for a large multinational corporation as an in-house consultant and knew the time had come for me to make my move when the company underwent some significant organizational changes. The fact that my former boss immediately hired me as an outside consultant provided a safety net for the short term. I knew if I was going to build and grow a business, however, that I was going to have to convince other clients I was worth hiring and other consultants my company was worth joining. To this end I embarked on a campaign to spread my passion to the world (or at least to the immediate business community).

My business expertise had grown over the years, and I had developed my own methods and procedures for helping companies improve their practices and increase their profits. I was filled with an intensity and a desire to share my theories and put them to work. On a personal level, I wanted to create a company where people could pursue their passions in a professional setting and feel good about what they were doing. Although I knew no company could be perfect, I also realized my company would be a microcosm for playing out my ideas and the first place potential clients would look to determine my credibility. After all, if I couldn't make things run smoothly in my company, how well could I instruct them on running theirs?

I was honestly so fired up about what I had to show my potential clients that they found it hard to resist me. Most were willing if not eager to give me a chance. Based on my experiences with the clients I had helped over the years through my various associations, my reputation had grown and supported the passion I exuded. During those days I ate, slept, and breathed continuous improvement. I still lived my life, but flashes of inspiration and motivation for making things better permeated my thoughts. I cannot say that passion was the sole cause of my success, but I do know that clients and employees recognized my enthusiasm and believed it was worth something. They invested in me with their finances and their futures even though I was entering uncharted waters. Without passion I might have eventually built a business, but the process would not have been as rapid, as smooth, or as successful.

Other companies have found passion to be the catalyst for progress and achievement. Chrysler sums up its product philosophy in one word: passion. They believe the challenge to building great cars is balancing technology and its inherent limitations with passion and its infinite possibilities. All top-level Chrysler executives must have a passion for automobiles. They must love what they build and long to build it better. The result is a product line that appeals to customers who are passionate about cars. These customers recognize passion in the design and develop a fierce loyalty to the manufacturer. In this way Chrysler's passion helps them not only design great cars but sell them too, which, after all, is the reason they are in business.

Pursuing your passion may have nothing to do with winning customers or attracting top-rate employees, but it has everything to do with reaching your Profit. Whether your Profit is measured in dollars or degrees of satisfaction, others can help get you there with fewer obstacles and greater joy. If you are committed to your passion and are prepared to make it an essential force in your life, share it with those around you and prepare to be amazed by what ensues.

HELP OTHERS

An added benefit of sharing your passion, and one you might not consider, is that you can be an agent of discovery for others. Think back on your own experiences and the people who you have been eager to follow or support. How did they make you feel—about life and about yourself? Did they help you see possibilities you had not recognized before? Did they expand your horizons, inspire you to think bigger and better? Whether your inspiration is a parent, teacher, friend, or boss, the result is the same. By engaging in their passion and supporting their causes, you learn something about yourself. You respond to them because they stir up something inside you. They make you feel more alive and more vital. Through them you discover a window into your own passion.

One thing I find particularly intriguing about our attraction to passion in others is that it can inspire our own *temporary* bouts of passion. I am sure you have experienced this in your life. Often in school or at work we are confronted with a challenge that we must meet with the members of a team; it could be an assignment, project, or presentation. In these situations, if a member of the team is passionate about the task, we too become passionate. We feed off his or her enthusiasm and find ourselves sharing it. Sometimes this exposure results in the discovery that we too possess the same underlying passion. More often, however, once the project is completed, we find our interest wanes and realize that our passion was only a response to a specific situation or a specific person. I call this situational passion.

As you begin to integrate passion into your life, you might find that others are drawn to you because of the light that shines from within you—let's call it your passion halo. If you find yourself in such a situation, where you are the one who brings passion to the table, you can use the opportunity to alert others to their feelings. Although their devotion to your causes may really be devotion to you, you can help them recognize the passion they are feeling as a potential boon and encourage them to find their own internal sources. An attentive follower, once inspired, may well turn into an impassioned leader.

This was the case for a young woman who was born into horrific circumstances. Jennifer's mother was a schizophrenic and her father a drug addict. When she was an infant, her mother tried to kill her and was subsequently institutionalized. During her early years, the courts placed Jennifer in a series of foster homes and temporarily with her grandparents. Her father petitioned the court for custody of the little girl and, after falsifying a urine test, was named her guardian.

Jennifer's childhood was full of fear and anguish and devoid of hope. She grew up under the el train in a community of drug abusers, prostitutes, and gangbangers. Her father was so completely absorbed by drugs that he sold all their possessions, even her schoolbooks, to fund his habit. His girl-friend, a prostitute, contributed to the finances of the household by bringing her clients back to the apartment where little Jennifer hid in corners, afraid and ashamed. Often her father would grow desperate for money and rent the apartment to other junkies. It served as a safe haven where they could shoot up, snort, inhale, or ingest their chosen poison without fear of arrest. Jennifer would come home from school, never certain of who might be there and in what condition. Imagine the terror this must have brought her, a small child unable to defend herself against whatever common criminal or derelict her father had invited into her home, the one place she should have felt safe.

There were reprieves from her time at home, but they offered no comfort: her father rented her to neighbors and others who approached him. She served as an experiment for people who were considering having children or just wanted to see what having a child was like. When she wasn't the temporary property of someone else or being terrorized by her father in his drug-induced rages, she spent time in parks, at friends' houses, and at school—anywhere but home. She began working in junior high school to earn enough money to buy food, because her father kept none in the apartment. When she was fifteen her boyfriend bought her a microwave and installed an industrial lock on her door to keep her father away, but he was able to tear it down and steal the oven along with the food she kept hidden under her bed.

After witnessing her father overdose one too many times, Jennifer realized that she had to escape. Many of her friends had succumbed to the lure of the streets, and she did not want the life she saw modeled in her father and his peers. As she told me rather matter-of-factly, "it was not of my character." In an effort to find safety and stability, she moved in with her boyfriend but found neither. The relationship quickly grew abusive. When the beatings he inflicted became too much to bear, she fled to a battered women's shelter, where finally she was safe.

Her story could have ended there. She could have accepted her role as victim and eked out a meager existence, living in fear and regret, but something happened to change her. What she saw in the shelter did not sadden or frighten her, it infuriated her. She found herself among women who seemed resigned to their situation, as if somehow they deserved it. She knew that she would not go down so easily. Under the auspices of a subsidized employment program administered through the shelter, she took a part-time job at a local non-profit organization helping children who suffered from AIDS. She felt a special connection to the children because her father had recently contracted the disease.

One of the requirements of employment was that she take a leadership class. She left that class a changed woman. By studying the examples of other young people who had become leaders and effected change, Jennifer began to believe that she too could make a difference. She learned of the passion that had led others to make things happen and recognized it in herself. What she had qualified as anger was a response to her situation, but underlying it was something deeper—a passion for helping others in the same condition. As if set on fire by the idea that she could make a difference, she joined every organization she could find that would help her to help others. She felt the first step in the evolution of her passion was to share it with other young people. If she could show her peers how they too could find safety, then perhaps they could find the seeds of their own potential and become agents of change.

With the help of a mentor from one organization, Jennifer got an apartment of her own where she at long last enjoyed the freedom of autonomy with the luxury of safety. She describes the months she spent in that small, one-room space as one of the best times of her life. She was liberated—free to think, free to learn, and free to look to the future. She was amazed by how much she could do when she was not devoting her time to worry or fear. In the decade that has passed since she left home, she has accomplished more than most do in a lifetime. She has served on the Commission of Human Rights and Youth Advisory Council for her city government. She has delivered addresses, run workshops, organized rallies, and served in a myriad of political and humanitarian groups. At age twenty-five, she founded a youth organization that has received the praise and attention of officials across the country. Its mission is to teach young people how to effect change by becoming involved in government rather than fighting against it.

Jennifer has been profiled in magazines and on television as an inspiration for the underprivileged and a role model for us all. Her long-term goal is to become the mayor of her city, one of the largest in the United States, but in the short term she is seeking to build upon her basis of experience and knowledge before making the leap to political office. She believes she is a product of the dangerous environment she grew up in, that without the trauma of her early years and the anger it aroused she would not be who she is today. We could speculate whether her passion for helping others would have emerged if she had been born in the suburbs to affluent parents, but we would miss the point. Jennifer was the recipient of the passion of others: although she did not experience their passion firsthand, she was sufficiently inspired through reading of their accomplishments and learning of their examples to discover her own. In turn, she has helped countless others by spreading her passion. She has served as a witness that passion can deliver them from their environments and help them to build better lives.

SUSTAIN YOUR PASSION

One of the most pronounced effects of sharing your passion is that it helps you sustain it over the long term. The next chapter is devoted to persisting in your passion, but I mention it here as it relates specifically to dealing with others. You now know that when you exude passion, when you actively strive to build your life around it, others will be attracted to you. Some will share your underlying passion; others will share only your excitement. Regardless of the source of their enthusiasm, their shared commitment can help you. It can serve as a daily reminder of what you are striving to achieve, as well as a stimulus when facing challenges.

Think about it for a moment. Let's assume your passion has led you back to school and you are spreading your obligations between work, school, and home. How will you feel each day if your coworkers disapprove of your new venture, or if your spouse and children resent the time you are spending away from them, or if your professors question your commitment to your studies? How easy will it be for you to sustain your passion from week to week if you are constantly defending it from the criticism of others? Obviously, you will find it far easier to meet your various obligations and remain excited about them if the people surrounding you are excited for you, if they share your passion. Your boss might endorse your efforts as an improvement on your abilities; your family might take pride in your ambition; your instructors might admire your dedication. Their collective encouragement may be the extra incentive you need to excel in all areas. Their commitment to you, and to the directions your passion is taking you, can reassure you when you doubt yourself and revitalize you when things get difficult.

Which of these situations you find yourself in will largely be determined by your ability to share your passion with these people. If you can convince them that your efforts are important and worthwhile, whether through your commitment, ardor, or example, you will create your own passion lifeline. This has been the case with a friend who recently made dramatic changes in his life. Steve was happy in his job, but wanted more. He was working in finance and had reached a ceiling he could not break through if he did not return to school for a graduate degree. He decided the time was right to make a change.

Steve approached his boss and was thrilled when she extended her support. He was nothing short of shocked when a few days later she told him the company would pay for his graduate degree if he remained under their employ for two years following the completion of his academic program. This seemed like the perfect scenario: he could keep his job and receive a free education at the same time. He soon realized, however, that the offer came with strings attached.

Steve's greatest commitment was to his family, and prior to his announcement his boss had been reasonably understanding about his need to curtail his hours to be with his wife and two small children. He never left before the workday was officially over, but there was an unspoken rule that the members of his team were expected to work well into the evening. Though his boss sometimes allowed him to leave in time to eat an evening meal with his family, she had not understood or supported the time he spent as a member of the lay clergy of his church. His position required him to spend one night per week at the church in addition to Sundays, but she felt this was just too much. She knew that the evening classes he was planning on taking would reduce his availability even further, so she put forth an ultimatum: something must go. Because it obviously wasn't going to be work or school (she supported him in these areas), it had to be church or family. Surely he could drop his position at the church, or tell his wife that she could sacrifice some of what little time she had with him for the good of his education.

Steve's response was immediate. He quit. He was not willing to abandon either of these things that meant so much to him, regardless of the price tag his boss tried to place on them. He knew that jobs would come and go, but that the human connections in his life were far too valuable to compromise. He did not want to let his family or his congregation down. Moreover, he knew that his heart could not be in his studies if he lost the respect or support of his friends and family. His boss was shocked and accepted his resignation anything but gracefully. She made his last few weeks at the company thoroughly unpleasant and did not wish him well when he left for the last time.

Steve realized that anyone who placed such restrictions on his passion to progress was not really supportive of it. His boss's motives in supporting him had had nothing to do with him personally. She had seen a way to help the company and herself, not Steve. After a month of searching, Steve found a new employer who was enthusiastic about him and his passion. He recognized that Steve's desire to improve would manifest in the quality of his work. Granting him the flexibility he needed to earn his degree (which he had decided to pay for himself) was a worthwhile investment. Steve's wife supported the changes he had made and was eager to help him make his way through school. She knew it would require a sacrifice on her part, but was glad to provide her support. He could attend school on his own terms and for his own reasons.

Steve learned that being open with his passion was the best way to win the support of those around him. He knew that given the state of his life and the people involved, he would rely on their encouragement to help him through an unusually busy and stressful time. Although his passion was the source of his initiative, the cooperation and understanding of those around him would ensure that he could continue on the course he had set.

Though we do not need others to agree with every decision we make or hold our hands as we follow our Passion Plan, their support and encouragement are valuable aids in our progress. Those with whom we have shared our passions and who support us in our pursuits can help in many times and in many ways. When we fall prey to our weaknesses, they can help us overcome them. When we lose sight of our Profit, they can help us focus on it. When we are confused by our options, they can help us understand them. A supportive

Passion Review

Do not be afraid to share your passion with others. The benefits are well worth the effort. By spreading your passion you will . . .

- Create a positive perception of yourself in others
- Accomplish your objectives
- Help others
- Sustain your passion

spouse, a nurturing mentor, a concerned friend—all can aid us on our road to Profit. To lay the groundwork for this future support, be sure to share your passion with those who are most important to you. Include them in your plans, seek their input, and welcome their advice. Lean on them when you need strength and turn to them when you need rejuvenation. What your passion cannot provide you—love, adulation, counsel—they can. If they know where you are going and why, they will help you sustain your passion and follow it to great ends.

TIPS FOR SPREADING YOUR PASSION

As you begin to follow your action plan, you will find many opportunities to spread your passion not only with those you love but with others who can help you in different ways.

Those who will give you professional opportunities—who will support your future ventures, buy your future products, and seek your future expertise—will be waiting for you to reach them. Those who will teach you, advise you, and learn from you will likewise be out there somewhere, ready to come into contact with you. The impression you leave, the example you set, and the excitement you inspire will all rely on your ability to convey your passion to them. You can take many steps to win others over to your cause.

First, realize that when you enter the world brimming with passion you will receive very different responses from the people around you. Some will be thrilled for you and eager to support you, others may begrudge your energy and secretly hope you will fail. Some will rush to follow you and others will try to block your way. There will be those who are refreshed by your outlook and others who laugh at your seeming naïveté. There will be those who believe in you completely and those who question your chances of success.

When you wear your passion on your sleeve, it is almost as if you are a missionary and everyone around you a potential convert. By following your passion openly and without regret, you expose yourself simultaneously to the scorn and derision of skeptics and the warmth and acceptance of believers. Not everyone will be won over to the changes you are trying to make. Some will respond immediately, as the passion you exude strikes a chord in them. Others will require patient convincing, their faith in you increasing gradually as you demonstrate your commitment and ability. Others will oppose you and require an even greater effort on your part. If time and performance do not prevail, then you might find it easier and healthier to leave them in your past, by filling the present with people who are in harmony with your personal Passion Plan.

Whatever the case may be, here are a few things you can remember when introducing or reintroducing passion into your life that will help you influence others in a positive way.

Be Enthusiastic

The enthusiasm that naturally emerges when we follow our passions will be your greatest resource in winning supporters for your Plan. It will make you stand out and it will be intriguing to others. So many people today feel drained of energy that they are automatically drawn to those who exude it. Though you don't want to be a novelty, don't be afraid to capitalize on your excitement. Smile, laugh, talk quickly, jump up and down, whatever you feel compelled to do. Your example will be refreshing and engaging.

The best evidence I had of the power of enthusiasm took place at a youth conference where a panel of speakers shared messages of encouragement and inspiration with the teenagers in the audience. Each speaker had an interesting story to tell, but none seemed to arouse much response. The audience sat quietly, not wanting to appear disrespectful, and at the same time struggling not to yawn. Then the final speaker took the stage. She was a thin, petite woman clad in blue jeans and a sweater. As she moved almost silently to the podium I could read their expressions. Based on her diminutive appearance, they expected a timid, soft-spoken, and probably boring speaker, but what they heard was anything but dull. From the moment she opened her mouth, this woman proved a bundle of energy. She was ebullient. Her speech was rapid, yet clear and emphatic. Her face was lively, changing expressions quickly as she moved from sentence to sentence. At first she tried to restrict her arms by tucking her hands securely in her back pockets, but soon she was gesticulating wildly in illustration of her story.

Initially the audience was amused. But their opinion quickly changed as they listened. They realized she was bouncing up and down not because she was weird but because she was so excited by what she was saying. She was telling them of difficult times with her parents and how she had resolved her problems. Within minutes they were sharing her pain and jubilation, wincing and laughing alternatively. Through her unadulterated emotion, she connected to the audience in a way the other speakers had not. Her energy struck a chord in them and opened their hearts and minds to what she was saying. For the first time that evening they actually listened.

If this woman had hidden her passion or tried to tone it down, her message might easily have been lost. But she had the courage and foresight to spread her enthusiasm rather than stifle it. Because she was willing to express her fervor, her words carried more weight and her message seemed more important, more honest. In the same way, you should not hesitate to let your passion show. Dare to be enthusiastic and others will notice.

Be Genuine

The reason this woman's energy was so convincing was because it was genuine. When I encourage you to be enthusiastic, I am not suggesting that you become a cheerleader and shout hurrah at every turn. Your exhilaration will be only as moving as it is authentic. We can detect when people really care about what they are doing or saying, and are easily alienated if they seem artificial. We dislike hollow performances and empty renditions, contrived stories and phony displays. If the woman I mentioned had been delivering an address on actuarial tables (something for which I assume she lacks passion), the same techniques would have proved futile—funny perhaps, but certainly not powerful or lasting.

Do not walk with a spring in your step unless it's really there. Don't act giddy unless your emotions give you no choice. If you are normally a calm and collected person, your passion might manifest in calm and collected ways. Do whatever feels right for you, but do not be reluctant to show others how passionate you are. When they sense your honesty, they will also sense your promise.

Don't Erect Barriers

By creating and following your action plan, you are changing your life. As you make this change, be careful not to place limitations on yourself that might prevent you from fully embracing your passion. If you erect barriers between the life you have now and the life you seek, you not only make things harder on you, you prevent others from reaching out to help you. I know a man who longed to be a screenwriter. Having reached his late twenties and not yet knowing how to break into the business, he quit his job, packed up his car, and headed to Los Angeles. He knew that before he could write, he had to read, so he applied at production companies all around the city for reader positions. (Readers are people who read and summarize screenplays submitted to movie studios.) He could not find a paying position, but convinced one company to let him work for free. Within months, he had his own office and a salary. Within two years, he was a production executive who had the authority to decide which scripts the company would buy and produce.

Talent was a requisite for his promotion, but passion was the reason he received attention. When he offered to work without compensation, the woman who hired him recognized not desperation but enthusiasm. The fervor with which he then approached his work gained the notice not only of his boss but of those who worked around him. They grew to respect his judgment and value his opinions, but would never have done so if he had not worked to tear down the barriers that could have stood between him and his dreams. He did not let inexperience, fear of rejection, or stubbornness interfere with his quest. He could have made excuses or backed down in the face of a challenge, but he chose to share his passion and help others give him the opportunities he needed to progress.

Be Consistent

Consistency, though difficult to achieve, is one of the surest ways to win the respect and support of others. Not consistent grumpiness, of course, but consistent passion will endear you to friends and family. Not that you have to be intense and excited every second, but you must remain committed to your passion and seek to pursue it from day to day. If you are erratic about it, others might question your motives or doubt your desire.

Certainly you will have high and low points and may need the help of others. If, however, you abandon your efforts one week and embrace them the next, those around you will be less likely to believe you are capable of working toward your goals, much less reaching them.

Be Supportive of Others

Finally, passion is not selfish. It is your own, but you should share it. And you can share the passion of friends and family just as they share yours. If your friend is taking up tennis to play out his passion for competition, don't criticize him or act apathetic. Encourage him, practice with him, attend matches together. Understand that just as your passion is integral to your happiness, so is the passion of others important to theirs. By supporting others in this way, you build a community of potential contributors to your personal Passion Plan.

 Passion Review

When pursuing your passion, you have the power to influence others in a positive way. As you follow your heart, remember to . . .

- Be enthusiastic
- Be genuine
- Don't erect barriers
- Be consistent
- Be supportive of others

Passion Review

To spread my excitement I will . . .

- Share my passion with others so that I may grow in it
- Understand that I have the power to help others just as they have the power to help me
- Be enthusiastic, genuine, and consistent in pursuing my passion
- Avoid erecting barriers that will prevent me from spreading my passion
- Sustain my passion by sharing it with others

As you go about living out your Passion Plan, remember you are not in it alone. Be sensitive to the aid others can provide—the inspiration, the encouragement, and the vision—that sometimes might escape you. Know also that you can be instrumental in helping others carry out their passions. You can help to kindle the excitement and enthusiasm for living that we each possess but rarely use. You have the power to persuade and be persuaded, to give and to take. Do not be afraid to do both as you strive to bring your passion to life and to give it form and meaning.

As you deal with others when following your Passion Plan, remember the following points:

To help you begin to spread your passion, complete Worksheet #6. Be sure to list the qualities you want to display to others and the ways you can inspire them by sharing your passion. Target specific actions you can take to build passion in your relationships with others.

The vital support that others provide is only one valuable resource you have in sustaining your passion as you follow your action plan. In the next chapter I will show you how to stick by your plan and bolster your passion over the long term. Do not forget as you move forward that above all your passion is powerful: just as it has the power to persuade, so does it have the power to survive. Before you move on, remember to complete Worksheet #6.

PASSION PLAN WORKSHEET #6

Step 6: Spread Your Excitement	How
A. The Image I Need to Project to Others:	Describe the type of image you need to project to others that demonstrates your personal energy and commitment toward your passion. Consider the following: • Have I shared my emotions and things that are important to me with others? • Can those around me sense my personal energy about my passion? • Are others eager to spend time with me or to be involved in my activities that further my passion?
B. Ways I Can Inspire Others by Sharing My Passion:	Identify ways that you can inspire others through the sharing of your passion. Consider the following: • How have others in my life inspired me to pursue my passion? • What can I do to learn about someone else's passion?

Passion Plan Worksheet #6 (cont.)

B. Ways I Can Inspire Others by Sharing My Passion (cont.):	• How can my passion inspire others to pursue their passion? • What lessons learned can I share with others that will help inspire them to pursue their passion?
C. I Can Spread My Passion the Following Ways:	Incorporate ongoing actions to continue spreading your passion. When spreading your passion, remember the following: • Be enthusiastic • Be genuine • Don't erect barriers • Be consistent • Be supportive of others

CHAPTER 9

Step Seven
Stay the Course

Great works are performed, not by strength, but by perseverance.

SAMUEL JOHNSON

If you are like me, sometimes you have made pledges to yourself that you did not keep, resolutions that you forgot, and plans that you abandoned. When we make promises to ourselves—to lose weight, work harder, do better—we often lack the resolve and stamina to see them through. Often the reason is that we make them for the wrong reason or in the wrong way. When you live your Passion Plan, the results will be different. By looking to your heart for inspiration, the changes you make will be the right ones—those you truly desire and of which you are capable. You *will* have the wherewithal to make them because by enlisting your passion, you give yourself a natural advantage. You open up the inner reserves of motivation and enthusiasm you never knew you had. These hidden energies are the key to staying the course, even when things are difficult.

Although passion is a powerful force, it does not ensure

that things will go smoothly or even according to plan. In implementing your plan, you might encounter unforeseen challenges. How you respond to these challenges will determine whether you are able to keep passion at the center of your life or drop it as quickly as you adopted it. Above all you must be persistent. Otherwise your reacquaintance with passion will be brief and will fall into the category of opportunities lost and actions regretted.

THE PASSION STIMULUS

Passioneers love their lives, but they are subject to the same bouts of frustration that you are. They can be bogged down by details, irked by delays, and annoyed by inefficiencies. They can get tired, grow bored, and feel fatigued. They are neither perfect nor superhuman. But they are superattuned to their hearts; as such they are able to overcome such problems. The critical difference between passioneers and others is that they understand how to look to their passion for renewal rather than escape. Passion actually revives and refreshes them.

Think about how passion might work in your own life. Imagine that you work in a job that does not elicit your passion. Let's go so far as to say you really dislike your work. Whether you are taking steps to change jobs or not, your days will be markedly different depending on whether passion is present in other areas. You might count the minutes at the office, waiting for the workday to end, only to come home feeling drained or depressed. You might then collapse into bed or sit numb before the television before starting the same routine the next morning. If, however, you are passionate about ballroom dance and fill your evenings with classes, rehearsals, and competitions, you might get more excited as the workday draws to a close and come home eager for the night's activities.

In this case, it might be a stretch to argue that the passion of your evenings could carry over and inspire you at work, but stranger things have happened. Think about a time you fell in love. Did time blur between meetings with the object of your affections? Did you glide rather than stumble through activities, walk with a spring in your step or a gleam in your eye? How about when you won an award, landed an account, or got a top grade on an assignment? Did your elation spread into your everyday activities and help you flow through your days?

Passion is a stimulus. Find ways to engage it, and it can help you endure situations that are less than ideal. In the long term, as we gradually reorient our lives around passion, we can turn to it for the added initiative we need to stick by our decisions and continue moving toward our Profit.

KEEPING YOUR PASSION ALIVE

It is easy to get bogged down in details and forget why you made a choice. If you take a new job because it is in a field you are passionate about, you cannot let annoying tasks or a meddling boss rob you of your motivation for being there. If you turn your focus from your passion—your love of the field—to your irritations—your dislike of a particular coworker or assignment—you will rapidly lose your excitement for your work. Such intervening factors not only prevent you from engaging your passion but may also prompt you to forget or doubt it.

So you must stay close to your passion as you follow your plan, especially if it calls for intermediate steps directed at building or developing that passion. Suppose you have a nascent passion for architecture and begin to pursue it by taking a drafting class. If you become discouraged by the difficulty of the course or are intimidated by the instructor, you might be tempted to drop the class or abandon the field completely. If architecture is truly a passion for you, however, you need to remember that your love of design should be preeminent to lesser considerations. The obvious choice would be to change classes or seek extra help in developing your skills. Unfortunately, many of us would fall into the trap of allowing fear or self-doubt to squelch our passion. Most of us have done it before, and if we are not vigilant we will do it again.

So relish your passion, and keep it special. Your goal should be to bring it into your everyday life, but not into the realm of the ordinary. It merits a position of reverence in your thinking because it holds the key to your better, happier self. Do not question or disparage it when things are difficult or confusing. And always remember to take the time and effort necessary to keep it alive.

Just how you do this depends on your particular passion and how you are working it into your life. Consider John, who as a boy was passionate about nature and about creating things. He longed to understand life, not only the chemistry and biology of living things but their forms and construction. He loved to draw and used pens and brushes to render his interpretations of life, which emphasized the beauty and intricacy of its structures.

When John got to college, he selected bioengineering as

his major. It seemed the perfect field to address his love of living things and his desire to create. But it disappointed him. Rather than building or designing things, he spent most of his time studying textbooks and memorizing facts. He approached one of his professors at the beginning of his senior year and finally asked, "When do we get to make something?" The reply disheartened him: "John, you obviously don't understand science. It is not about creating things, it's about analyzing them." After digesting that, he felt a renewed resolve to pursue his passion in a different way. It was too late to change his major from science to art, but not too late to minor in art. And he could switch his science major specialty from bioengineering to zoology, still graduating on time but focusing on the science of life from a different perspective.

Many of us would not have been so determined. All those changes meant much more work and much less free time for John. A more pragmatic man might have put his passion on the back burner for nine months until graduation and then sought employment in a more inspiring field, but he was not willing to make that compromise. Those nine months were too precious. He viewed them as an opportunity to explore and learn as much as he could about his passion and its applications before entering the working world. Ironically, when he made the change his adviser counseled against it. He suggested a switch to mechanical engineering, a field that offered better job prospects than the more impractical combination of zoology and art.

John was not swayed. He immersed himself in his studies, concerned about his future employability but bolstered by his sheer enthusiasm for the material. "It was as if my passion was driving me to a place where others had not been," he said. "I did what was inside me, what I had to do." As his adviser had anticipated, John found few opportunities for work. What is out there for the zoologist-artist? Whatever he did, he knew it must address his dual love for science and art—his passion for the powers of creation.

And because of that, John is now a success. The first position he considered was as quality control technician for a cookie company. It did involve both art and science; he'd have to assess the visual quality of the cookies and ensure their culinary standards. He decided against it, as he did a job selling ads in the Yellow Pages (even though, he thought momentarily, art could be viewed as communication and science as technology).

The opportunity John sought and quickly accepted was as technician in a medical school laboratory. Working in the Department of Anatomy, he headed the group that prepared specimens, models, and exhibits for professors. What a perfect blending of his passions! His task was not just to prepare the materials, but to do so in a way that would make them communicate to people. They had to be visually accessible and engaging. He felt that the students' ability to learn from them was directly proportional to their aesthetic value.

Working in the lab, John's passion rose further primarily because of one man: the professor who oversaw the lab, a world-renowned scientist and remarkable human being. He showed John that science is really about discovery and creation, the fervent pursuit of understanding and inspiration, and that like art it requires feeling and observation and offers unlimited potential for exploration. John learned that there is art to science and a science to art. The professor's views were a revelation to him. He felt his passions validated and his mission bolstered.

John carried his renewed enthusiasm directly into the art department of the university, where he studied under a man he describes as "one of the fathers of industrial design." From this professor, he learned of the potential for marrying technology and aesthetics not in relation to life but to things. He was inspired by the idea that the design of functional objects—telephones, tractors, and trains—could elicit emotional responses from those who used them. Moreover, emotion was not only an outcome of design but a necessary ingredient in the creative process. He understood that architecture, art, and technology all exemplify the passion of their creators.

After earning his master's degree in fine arts, John decided he wanted to spread his vision and understanding to others. He wanted young people to understand that art and science are not exclusive, that they need not choose one at the expense of the other. He secured a professorship at a state university, where he started an interdisciplinary major that encompassed business, engineering, and science. His work gained the notice of a few large corporations that promptly hired him as a consultant to design various products for them. This work hit a chord that resonated deep within, and in his own words, "he has been designing things ever since."

Not everyone was thrilled by John's challenge to tradition, however, and he was denied tenure four years after joining the university. Rather than remaining in an environment where he felt his passion would be stifled, he left the school. What was a risky decision became a beneficial move as another university almost immediately approached John. Though he remained at the new school for only one year, his time there allowed him to further refine his professional ambitions. He now knew that design had to be at the heart of his work.

After a stint as director of design for a local resort, John and a friend started their own design firm. John was prompted to take this step for many reasons. He wanted to explore his passion through the medium of buildings. He also felt he could add something unique in a region where architects viewed their work as that of technicians rather than artists. He received his certification as an architect and worked for more than ten years designing residences and commercial buildings. Just as he had sought to evoke an emotional response in consumers through the design of industrial products, so he attempted to create buildings that would inspire the people who used them.

John built upon his skills, but after a time found that his work no longer stimulated or excited him. He had learned a lot and grown a lot, but he knew there was something more he should be doing. He felt "that little itch" so many passioneers do when their lives move out of alignment with their passions. He wanted to use his expertise and enthusiasm to create something more daring and more unconventional than the traditional building market in his state was prepared to accept. So he told his partner he was finished and signed over his interest in the partnership. Simple as that.

Again John took what at the time must have seemed a considerable risk. He had a wife and four children, and as such a steady income was a necessity. He and his wife agreed, however, that he needed to continue testing the limits of his potential and find work that would allow him to grow as an artist and an individual. The family's financial security had always been predicated on John's passion, and now was no time to break the pattern. So he investigated his options and found himself drawn to the theme-park industry.

After turning down an offer from one of the industry giants, John applied for a position with the company of a famed Hollywood producer. The company was creating an attractions division and hoped to open a series of its own theme parks based on the work of the producer. Though competing against candidates more skilled and experienced than he, John landed the position on the basis of his passion. He exuded a confidence, commitment, and excitement that the producer found hard to resist. When John had worked for others in the past, he was discouraged by their unwillingness to let him freely exercise his imagination and creativity. In his new position, he was encouraged to experiment, and the company gave him an unqualified vote of confidence. Whatever he decided to do was what they would do.

John defines this experience in his life as a "major eye-opener." At long last he realized that his particular creativity— his ardent desire to understand his environment and at the same time create it—was truly the cornerstone of his professional and personal life. A deeply religious man, he credits both his passions and his abilities to God, but on a secular level, he has built his successes around his devotion and unwavering commitment to them. At the time he realized his passion was no different than it had been under the direction of past employers, only that the perception of it had changed. He could unleash his passion and follow it to new heights regardless of how others valued his work. Certainly their support was helpful, but his passion could endure without it.

Three years after hiring John, the production company abandoned its attractions division, a development that, once again, John could have viewed as a stumbling block. Instead he grew excited by the prospects of using his newly gained expertise to build his own business. The business the company was giving up, he would gladly accept. Today John has built an incredibly successful home-based business and has designed theme parks and attractions around the world. He is currently working on a book that will address the psychology of our attraction to theme parks and the experiences we seek by visiting them. He is a gifted and fascinating man who has created a rich and fulfilling life around his passion.

John is exceptional, but the challenges he faced are typical—confusion surrounding his passion and its applications, frustration at the advice offered by others, uncertainty in the face of change, and temptation to take a safer, less fulfilling course through life. He was fortunate to recognize his passion early though he did not always understand it. He is to be admired because he had the courage and the conviction to follow it when it would have been easier to abandon it. Time and time again, he looked to his heart for answers and recognized that he must persist in the pursuit of his passion to realize his potential and create his own happiness. He did not do so rashly or without thought to the consequences.

John compares his gradual process of self-realization to the flight of a bird that circles its home at greater and greater distances before finally migrating. The stimulus that prompted him to widen his horizons was the stirring within that he now identifies as his passion. Each time it gave him the strength to take the steps necessary to move closer to his Profit, and with each step he learned the value of perseverance.

FACING CHALLENGES

Opposition is the natural state of the universe. Though things can go smoothly, often they do not. As John learned, in the course of executing your plan you will probably face challenges. Things might be more difficult than you anticipated or not work out as you had hoped. You might face circumstances you did not consider or emotions you have never experienced. If your plan comes to fruition too easily you might feel unfulfilled or that you were mistaken in your expectations. If it is too great a struggle, you might question whether the risks outweigh the potential benefits. You can be prepared to face these challenges and to overcome them. The rest of this chapter helps you understand what you might encounter and how you can respond to ensure not only that your passion survives but thrives.

There are three basic strategies for handling impediments to your plan. The ones you choose should reflect your situation. If you question your ability to carry out your plan, consider taking the following actions:

- Modifying your action plan
- Heightening your commitment
- Reevaluating your passion

Before making any changes, reflect on the source of your problems. Do they come from within—insecurity, fear, doubt—or from the outside world—rejection of your ideas, opposition to your actions, lack of opportunity? If the answer lands clearly in the external category, your first step should be to revisit your plan and modify it to meet your current situation. If your struggles are mainly internal, determine whether they are a response to pushing yourself outside your comfort zone or an indication that your passion is not as strong as you thought it was. If you are confident in your passion but tentative about change, renew your personal commitment to your plan. If your passion is wavering, it may not have been a passion to begin with. Consider each of these alternatives in greater depth.

Modifying Your Action Plan

If passion is the cornerstone of your plan, flexibility must be the framework. Because you cannot predict the future with perfect accuracy, there is a good chance you will need to modify your plan as you follow it. Adaptations and revisions are a necessary part of your action plan so you should not be discouraged if this is the case. Instead you should view changes to your plan as improvements rather than admissions of failure. The life you are constructing from your passion can assume many forms. If you want to build the Eiffel Tower, do not be afraid to build Notre Dame if someone offers you stained glass instead of iron.

The changes you need to make could be the result of many factors. Perhaps you were too ambitious in setting your scope, intensity, or pace and need to slow things down. Maybe you are prepared to act more aggressively than at first and need to intensify your efforts. Perhaps you have found new opportunities or revised your thinking regarding old ones. You might, upon entering a new phase of your life, find that your purpose has changed and so, therefore, change the way you pursue your passion.

All this sounds good in theory, but it might be difficult to consider your challenges as opportunities. As an entrepreneur I know all too well the ups and downs of starting and running a business. It can be stressful, especially when struggling to keep a company afloat. For many who feel a lifelong passion to create businesses, failure is a part of life, a marker along the road to eventual success. To the diehard entrepreneur the demise of one endeavor often means the birth of another. I know of a man who opened and closed three software companies before the fourth finally succeeded. In retrospect he realizes that the failure of the first three only fueled his passion to build the fourth. Certainly he would have preferred that the earlier businesses succeeded, but the fact that they did not did not dispel his passion. He simply changed his plan to accommodate new ways of pursuing it.

You too can reach such a level of confidence and comfort with your passion. If you seek diligently to listen to your heart and to weave threads of passion into your life, you will gain the critical understanding that the process of experiencing passion can be as fulfilling as reaching your goals. As you find this to be true, your ability to carry out your plan will increase. You will also begin to anticipate situations that might require you to alter your plan and become more adept at making changes. Your success in facing challenges and adapting to them will have a cumulative effect. The energy you derive from one experience will carry over into the next and give you the self-assurance to continue in the face of opposition, criticism, or confusion.

Heightening Your Commitment

If the challenges you face are coming not from outside but from within you, consider how committed you are to your Passion Plan. In Chapter Three I discussed the internal forces that prevent so many of us from discovering our passions—self-doubt, fear, paralysis, numbness, procrastination, caution. These forces are just as detrimental once we put a name to our passion. They do not evaporate once we decide to follow it; they just fade into the background, where they wait for us, in moments of weakness, to invite them back.

If you question your worthiness or ability, then the solution to your struggles may not be simple, but it is straightforward. Heighten your commitment to your passion. Do whatever it takes to reassure yourself that you can build a life around passion and that you deserve the happiness it will bring. This might seem difficult if you are tentative or remain unconvinced, but until you believe in yourself and the power of your passion you cannot expect to make a lasting change. You might find the added strength you need in the counsel of others, in your imagination, or in the example of those who have done what you hope to do. For every weakness you possess, someone else has overcome it a hundredfold. There is no reason that your passion cannot take you where you want to be. Once you accept that and are able to cast off your personal demons, you will be able to follow your Passion Plan with confidence and without regret.

The surest way to overcome your doubts and fears is to experience your passion—not to define it or speculate on its possibilities, but to actually feel it. Nothing can build your faith in yourself like a passion high. If your plan involves making difficult changes in the present so that you can experience your passion in the future, then do it now. The more familiar you become with it and the more often you exercise it, the more confident you become and the closer you move toward realizing your Profit. If you view your peak experiences not as aberrations from the norm but as glimpses of your underlying potential, you will see that you are capable of much more than you give yourself credit for.

Reevaluating Your Passion

If nothing else seems to be working and you cannot find encouragement in passion-related experiences, you may need to reevaluate the passions you are pursuing. It might well be that what you have defined as a passion really is not. This is understandable and not uncommon. Often our memories distort our feelings and our desires cloud our judgment. We may identify something as a passion only because we wish it was or thought it was before.

I have a friend who played tennis competitively from age seven through college. She was talented and could have sought a career as a professional athlete but chose to attend college and continue tennis only as a hobby. After college she was so busy building a career and a family that she dropped tennis altogether. Often she mused on her tennis days and longed to play again. Tennis was, she thought, a passion sorely missing from her life. When finally she resumed playing at age thirty, she found she was mistaken. She enjoyed the lessons she was taking, but found they did not bring the exhilaration she previously associated with the sport. When she thought about her tennis experience, she realized that her feelings were more likely connected to the people she had trained with and the relationships they had shared rather than the tennis itself. After suffering a few minor injuries, she quit her classes, understanding that tennis would always be an enjoyable avocation but never a passion.

How can this be? If passion is the great liberator of our potential and the truest reflection of our inner selves, how can we be mistaken about it? Shouldn't our passions be clear to us once we understand what they are and how they make us feel? Yes, but even many educators who know passion in their own lives are amazed by students who do not know what to hope or yearn for. They are missing that necessary ingredient in the passion formula: wanting. A passion is something you long to do and need to do in order to feel complete. Until you've felt it, you cannot imagine it; you can only sense its absence.

Digging through the emotions of your past or foraying into the uncharted territory of emotions unknown to you is difficult work. Suppose you think it would be romantic to be

Passion Review

To keep your passion alive you need to stay close to it and keep it special. If you face a challenge in carrying out your action plan, you may need to do one or more of the following:

- Modify your action plan
- Heighten your commitment
- Reevaluate your passion

an environmentalist or exciting to be a business tycoon. You cannot know either to be true unless you try. You can only speculate about what you have not experienced. If after introducing something new into your life you realize it is not a source of passion, do not hesitate to return to the discovery phase of the plan and begin again to look for possibilities. Though it can be discouraging to move three steps forward only to take two steps back, take heart in the one step you gained along the way: recognizing the need and potential for passion in your life. If you need to start over, do so with high hopes and good spirits. What you learned the first time around will almost certainly benefit you the next.

RENEWING YOUR PASSION

Most of us, though we may suffer from periodic bouts of confusion, are aware on some level of our passions. Once we identify and begin to follow them, we can expect moments of weakness. Just because our commitment wanes or our confidence falters does not mean our efforts are without merit or made in vain. Sustaining your passion is a challenge to be expected, but you can prepare to meet this challenge by building certain controls into your action plan. Most important you must recognize that persistence is about renewal. If you can continuously reaffirm, replenish, revitalize, and reawaken your passion, you *will* be able to stay the course.

You might think this a tall order, especially if you've only recently begun to follow your passion. Try to think of renewal not as a daunting duty but as a welcome luxury. You can reenergize daily by indulging your passion and at the same time ensure its continued influence in your life. The concept of indulgence is an important one. Sometimes we get so intimidated by the magnitude of the changes we are trying to make that we forget the reason we are making them: we want to be happy. Remembering this, consider incorporating the following into your daily routine.

Create Goal-Based Scenarios

The best way to feed your passion is to create opportunities to excel using it. We love affirmation of our efforts in the form of praise from others and pride in ourselves. As such you must set immediate goals for yourself that will enable you to utilize your passion and evaluate its effectiveness. If you have taken up running, your goal could be to reach a certain distance or place in a given race. You could say you run for the pure joy of the experience, and perhaps you do feel exhilarated when running. While this may be true, your impetus for continuing to run and continuing to develop your passion will hinge on the sense of accomplishment you build while doing it. If you do not put any measures into place, you will not have a sense of your progress.

Would you prefer getting an "A" in a class where everyone was guaranteed the grade just by showing up, or in a class where you did your best work and were rewarded for it? Would you feel more motivated to continue painting if you had ten works in progress or one completed canvas? Which would you share with others as an expression of your efforts? Would you feel more likely to train harder if you played in a tournament that was held just for the fun of it or one that crowned a champion?

I am not suggesting that passion is necessarily about competitiveness or winning awards. I merely mention it to highlight our need to feel our actions are getting results, whether they are measured with ribbons and trophies, promotions and raises, smiles and thanks, or pride and satisfaction. When you know you are working toward a goal, when there is a challenge to be met, you are more likely to rise to the occasion and perform at your best than when there is no deadline to be met or no task to be completed.

As you follow your passion, then, be sure to seek opportunities that provide quantifiable results. If you are engaging it at work, take on projects, set deadlines, and seek feedback from your boss. If you are pursuing it at leisure, find peers or mentors to evaluate your progress, join leagues or clubs that provide structure and support, and set performance goals for yourself. When you receive confirmation that your efforts are worthwhile, you are strengthened in resolve and heightened in spirit. Your path to Profit, rather than being a long, arduous trek, can be a series of strolls (or sprints if you are in a hurry). You can travel from accomplishment to accomplishment, milestone to milestone, each time drawing renewed energy and commitment from your successes.

Make the Tough Decisions

We love to be rewarded—for hard work, for a job well done, for trying our best. We can receive praise and acclaim as a result of our everyday activities, but the greatest rewards come with risk: the greater the risk, the greater the potential reward. When building our lives around passion, we cannot expect to get too far too fast unless we are willing to take chances. We take an immediate risk by investing our time and our energy in our Passion Plans when both are such precious commodities. The greater risk comes though when we open ourselves to criticism and possibly failure. If we fall short of the goals we profess, we might lose respect, faith, or confidence. If, however, we prevail in our efforts, then the pride of our accomplishment increases. You probably know how this feels. Someone tells you you won't be able to do something because you lack skill or talent or courage. You want more than anything to prove to them and to yourself that you can. If you actually prevail in your efforts, your success is even sweeter than if they had believed in you to begin with and you are strengthened for meeting your next challenge.

Sometimes the risks we take extend beyond our pride into the realm of security and privilege. Embracing our passion often means giving up what is safe—our salaries, our habits, our perceptions. Because we have to see things differently to approach them differently, pursuing the Passion Plan forces us to reevaluate the importance of the things that are comfortable for us. As we do so we learn that what is familiar is not necessarily nurturing or beneficial to us in the long term. You will not be able to persist in your passion if you do not make the difficult decisions that move you away from the comforts that weaken your passion and toward those that empower it. This could mean giving up a paycheck from a job you dislike, abandoning the familiarity of zoning out rather than honing in, or challenging the safety of emotional restraint. Each time you make a choice informed by your passion you reaffirm its importance in your life and renew your commitment to it. These decisions do not have to be made hastily or without planning, but they do need to be made. The survival of your passion relies on it.

Accept Change

We are curious creatures. Just as quickly as we can change our lives for the better, we can abandon the progress we have made and revert to our former weaknesses. A necessary part of bringing passion into your life is *allowing* it to stay there. To do this you need to accept that changes once made are worth preserving. If passion is truly at work in your life, this should be a welcome admission; but if you cling to the past despite its imperfections, you will find it hard to keep moving forward. As much as you need to be vigilant in building a passion-filled life, you also need to relax and relish changes once they occur. Take pride in your accomplishments and acknowledge their importance. Don't be reluctant to accept what is new; instead understand that today's change can be tomorrow's reality.

Turn to Others for Support

Your passion must come from within, but support can come from all around you. As discussed in Chapter Eight, those we live with, work with, and play with can help us remain firm in our pursuits. If you experience a setback or dwindle in your resolve, look to those who believe in you for encouragement. They can help you remember why you sought change and why you are capable of achieving it. You can also take heart from those who have been where you are and have confronted the same challenges. They can renew your confidence while providing a fresh perspective on your plan.

Take Perspective Breaks

You might remember when I discussed discovering your passion that taking time away from your normal activities, from the demands of your everyday life is one of the best ways to get in touch with your passions. Once you are aware of them, it is equally important that you take such breaks to reinforce them. The dangers of our hustle-bustle lifestyles can creep into our lives just as they did before we began following our Passion Plans. If we devote our energies to following checklists, charts, and time frames, we might easily forget what prompted us to create them. To prevent yourself from losing the spirit of your quest in logistics, take frequent opportunities to clear your head and listen to your heart. Take a solitary walk or drive (preferably in a peaceful setting), spend a few hours in silence, go to a place that stirs your soul. Before jumping back into your busy world, the hope and enthusiasm that inspired your plan will return. You will feel refreshed, renewed, and eager to press forward.

Follow Your Action Plan

Keeping your passion fresh means actively feeding it through thought, experience, and imagination. This means you must pursue it not just in word but in deed. In your action plan you have outlined the ways you will nurture your passion and develop it further, but the plan will do you little good unless you follow it. This might seem an obvious point to make, but you would be surprised how many people gain confidence in the early stages of executing their plans and then feel they can continue without following them. They grow complacent, assuming that things will work out for the best given their new attitude. While you need to be flexible and open yourself to opportunities that come your way, you also need to be taking steps to create them.

If I plan to open a restaurant someday, I cannot become too excited by my early successes as a chef, maître d', or entrepreneur—that I expect everything will fall into place when the time comes. Although entirely possible, this is a dangerous assumption. As I am building my expertise, I must also be thinking ahead to the future phases of my plan. A client might hear of my plans and approach me with a site, or I might have to spend months scouring the city with realtors to find one. I might have an inspiration as to the type of cuisine, or need to conduct extensive research to determine what kind the market will support.

 Passion Review

To keep your passion alive, you must seek to renew it daily. You can incorporate the following practices into your routines to help you do this:

- Create goal-based scenarios
- Make the tough decisions
- Accept change
- Turn to others for support
- Take perspective breaks
- Follow your action plan

I sincerely hope that you will benefit from what many describe as synchronicity, or the fortuitous and often mysterious workings of the world, but I cannot advise you to rest your future on it. Once you have created your plan, devote yourself to it. Revise it as needed, but do not forget or diminish its importance. You will be naïve to expect your passion to grow any more than you plan for it to.

RECOGNIZING BURNOUT

When we do too much too fast for too long we suffer from burnout. Following your action plan is no exception. If you are doing everything you know you should be but you've lost your enthusiasm either to frustration or exhaustion, you need to take a break. Don't get me wrong. It's not your passion at fault, just your methods of pursuing it. You might be putting too much pressure on yourself, or you might be doing things geared toward developing your passion that could actually be diminishing it. Remember, your passion is like a thread that you can weave in and out of your life as your feelings, circumstances, and opportunities suggest. Maybe now is not the time to go full guns, but rather a time to be low key in your pursuit. As long as you keep your passion near the surface, if you acknowledge it and nurture it in subtle ways, it will not abandon you. There will come a time when you will once again be ready to intensify your efforts and follow them to different, more fruitful ends. In the days that intervene you may gain a renewed appreciation for your passion and a fresh vision of the role it can serve in your life.

Passion Review

To stay the course I will . . .
- Commit to keeping my passion alive
- Acknowledge that things do not always go as I might hope or plan for
- Approach challenges as opportunities
- Set myself up to succeed
- Take steps to renew my passion on a daily basis
- Review my action plan as needed

Though the potential for negatives such as burnout and depletion exists, the greater likelihood is that you will be rejuvenated rather than drained by your passion. According to many doctors and medical researchers, the excitement and satisfaction that accompany our positive moods can boost our immunity, improve our health, and provide us with the energy to excel. Fueled by passion, you will be stronger, happier, and more resilient. You will be able to face the challenges that come your way and endure in your quest for a better, more fulfilling life. As you follow your Passion Plan, remember the following points.

Use Worksheet #7 to brainstorm ideas for keeping your passion alive as you carry out your plan. Imagine possible challenges and think of ways you might respond to ensure your passion survives.

You have now reviewed each of the seven steps of the

Passion Plan. You have not mastered them all (few ever do), but you should be well on the road to bringing about your own success, to reaching your personal Profit. You are now prepared to discover your passions, find ways and reasons to integrate them into your life, and sustain them over the long term. In the next chapter we revisit the concept of Profit and explore the ways achieving it will change your life.

PASSION PLAN WORKSHEET #7

Step 7: Stay the Course	How
A. Ways to Keep My Passion Alive:	Identify ways to keep your passion alive as you continue to pursue it. It's important to not let any initial challenges or difficulties discourage you. Consider the following: • What have I done to make my passion special in my life? • Have I taken the time and effort necessary to keep my passion alive? If not, what do I need to do differently? • Do I need to recommit to pursuing my passion? • Who can help me maintain my enthusiasm for my passion?
B. Possible Strategies for Facing Challenges to My Plan:	Develop strategies for handling challenges and impediments to your plan. If you find yourself questioning your ability to carry out your plan, consider the following: • Do I need to modify my plan?

Passion Plan Worksheet #7 (cont.)

B. Possible Strategies for Facing
Challenges to My Plan (cont.):

- Am I truly committed
  to pursuing my passion?
  If not, do I need to
  heighten my commit-
  ment?
- Are there signs that
  indicate that I need to
  reevaluate my passion?

CHAPTER 10

Profit with a Capital P
Reaping Your Rewards

Success is getting what you want; happiness is wanting what you get.
ANONYMOUS

When you picked up this book it was because you wanted something. You might not have been unhappy, you might not have been confused; but on some level you were searching for something more. It could have been as specific as more money or a new job, or as general as greater influence or increased happiness. Whatever it was, it constitutes your personal idea of Profit, or what I call Profit with a capital P. The capital letter signifies that the intended rewards are not just of abundance but also of enrichment. They fill us and have meaning for us. They don't merely add to our lives, they improve them. This then—Profit—is the expected consequence of your Passion Plan.

There are however, two types of Profit: that which you seek and that which you find. The things that you hope for in beginning your Passion Plan are the Profit you seek. The positive outcomes that result from following it are the Profit you find. Often the two are the same: we begin with a goal in mind, and we reach it. Just as often, though, they differ: we surprise ourselves by looking for one thing but finding another. Each type of Profit is vital to our fulfillment, because without dreams we cannot imagine our future and without results we cannot create it.

As you read these final pages, I want you to remember that with passion in your life, your Profit is well within reach. At the same time I want you to realize that the Profit you envision today will be the foundation from which you view a new or more complete Profit tomorrow. Profit after all is no more static than is passion. It is at once a concept and a reality, a motivation and an accomplishment. Think of it not as an end, but rather a beginning. Strive toward it knowing always that beyond it and within you there is more potential than you ever imagined.

THE PROFIT WE SEEK

As I explained in the beginning of this book, the value of passion is twofold: it improves the quality of our experience *and* it helps us get what we want out of life. But what is it that we want? While only you can answer this question for yourself, traditionally the things we have longed for have been banded together and packaged under the label of success." Wealth, position, power, and security once comprised the cornerstones of success, but this is no longer the case. As I have worked with countless individuals over the past twenty-five years, many of who have attained this time-honored version of success, I have learned that our definition has evolved to include more varied and less conventional characteristics. Though many of us desire some or all of the traditional elements, yesterday's success has given way to today's Profit, which at its core resides in internal meaning rather than external displays.

This change seems ironic in light of the increasing frenzy of our lives. So many of the things we do—racing from place to place, overloading on information, biting off more than we can chew—seem directed toward building what we no longer value or at least value less. Despite our deference to these habits, we are nonetheless finding ways to build upon our new concept of Profit. One of the most striking changes to sweep the late-twentieth-century landscape is the quest for freedom—not financial freedom per se, but freedom from bosses and bureaucracies, time clocks and cafeterias. We want to be self-sufficient, to work for ourselves or with our friends. Job security is, after all, a thing of the past, and self-employment gives us the flexibility our frenetic lives demand. The pervasiveness of these desires is reflected in the actions of many employers who are creating more flexible work environments that in turn promote greater freedom.

Because we have so little time for ourselves we have come to value economy of experience. In other words we want to make the most of our time because we have so little of it. This doesn't mean that we're not subject to bouts of television-induced vegetation, but we do seek to be judicious in juggling our limited amounts of this precious commodity between the gym, the office, and the living room. If we're going to make the effort to get to the gym, we'd better put in a good workout. If we're going to burn the midnight oil to complete a project on time, we'd better be recognized for our work. If we're going to read a book, it had better be a good one. I call this return on

time investment or ROTI. The greater our ROTI, the more satisfied we are with our experiences.

Return on investment is also the justification many people
provide for seeking careers that in some way reflect their skills
and personalities. If we are going to make the most of our work
experience, we should do something for which we have an
aptitude or ability. This may sound obvious, but career selec-
tion was not always a matter of preference. Often it was about
pragmatism or precedent. Work at the factory because it is
there, or because your father did. Be an accountant because it
is steady work. People often drew paychecks regardless of performance or expertise. With the occasional exception, this is
not the way of the world today. Competition is cutthroat,
clients are fleeting, and bosses are demanding. So why not
improve your chances and do something you're good at?

One of the upsides of these new definitions of Profit—
freedom, flexibility, maximum ROTI, greater work/life integration—is that they all point to passion as a means of achieving
it. They are a de facto recognition that life is too short and time
is too precious to be wasting it doing things that make us
unhappy or drain us of our vitality. We want meaning in our
experience and meaning comes from the heart.

This feeling reinforces our more romantic notions of Profit,
or those not confined by constraints of money or time. Many of
us want a firm spiritual grounding as well as a financial one. We
value the quality of our relationships rather than the quantity
and seek to make lasting connections rather than fleeting ones.
We long to make contributions to our families and communities that will make a difference to others and improve our
worth as members of humankind. We want to leave a legacy,
one that transcends trophies or dollar signs, one that witnesses

the potential greatness we alone possess. This is the Profit we seek above all.

THE PROFIT WE FIND

Ralph Waldo Emerson once wrote, "The reward of a thing well done is to have done it." Similarly, the greatest Profit that comes from living with passion is not the objectives that we meet but the experience of meeting them. In this sense, passion is its own greatest reward. To understand what I am proposing, think about it in these terms. If I were to tell you that no matter how hard you tried you could not reach your Profit, would you stop trying? Would your efforts, if they filled you with enthusiasm and excitement, if they gave you great joy and satisfaction, not be worth continuing regardless of the outcome? I have every confidence that you can achieve the Profit you envision; but as you do, be sure to appreciate the value of your passion, not as a means to an end, but as an end in itself.

Beyond the heightened level of experience that passion creates, there is another form of *immediate* Profit we gain by living with passion, and one you might not consider when focusing on your *future* Profit. It is the gradual self-awareness that comes with working toward your potential. Because your passion is a reflection of your individuality, once exercised, it enhances your unique sense of the world and your place in it. When Henry David Thoreau headed out to spend his months on Walden Pond, he stated that he did so so that he might never "be judged not to have lived." If we deny what is inside us, the passion that defines who we are, then we surely are bringing this same judgment upon ourselves. By not just acknowledging our passion but embracing it and following it, we don't just live our lives we define them.

Though you might not dwell on these types of Profit when creating your Passion Plan, they probably will not come as a surprise once they occur. They are, after all, foreseeable benefits of building a life around passion. What you might not expect, however, is to discover that what you wanted when you began, the Profit you envisioned, is not what you want now. Consider the example of a young software executive who viewed his ultimate Profit as an early retirement. When I say early, I mean at the age of thirty-five! He was certain that if he could achieve this goal, then his life would be perfect and somehow complete. Free of the shackles of work, he could ski, surf, travel the world, or just sit at home—in other words do whatever he wanted to do. He reached thirty-five and sure enough, thanks to a bounty of stock options, he was able to leave his job.

This young man soon found that retirement was not the thrill he had thought it would be. It wasn't that he was bored, rather that something was missing. He realized that despite what he had previously thought, work was one of the things he wanted to do most. He was passionate about technology, competition, and progress, and his former employer had proved a climate in which these passions had thrived. Suddenly eliminating his job from his life had created a passion void he was finding difficult to fill. Needless to say he returned to work to an employer who felt privileged to have him.

Another retiree from the same industry left her position with dreams of being the ideal mother to her two small children. Given freedom from professional obligations and with a multimillion-dollar portfolio, she figured she could give them everything they ever needed—her love, her time, her talents, and any material possession she could imagine. As she had expected she loved being a full-time mother. Unexpectedly though she discovered a new desire. She realized that she and her husband had more money than they or their children would ever need. She felt a strong urge to do something more with the money than letting it grow in bank accounts or mutual funds, so she decided to put it to work for others. She created a philanthropic family trust and spent her free time researching charities to determine where the trust would make its donations. Money, something she had never defined as Profit, brought her both a Profit she had longed for—retirement—and one she had not—charity.

This illustrates the elusiveness of our desires. We never really know what we want because we cannot imagine how we would feel if we had it. We focus on what we think we want because we have no alternative. Unless we guess we have nothing to work toward. As the woman I mentioned learned, a Profit once realized can reveal another you might not have anticipated. In the alternative, as the man learned, what we imagine as Profit might seem meaningless once we achieve it. Like many of us I'm sure he chose retirement as his goal because it was what it *seemed* he should want. But as Shakespeare cannily observed, if we pursue an end for idle reasons, often it "hath in it no profit but the name."

Sometimes it is hard to discern the longings of our heart from the promptings of the world, but as you grow stronger in your passion you will gain a better sense of what really matters to you. As you grow accustomed to the confidence and inspiration that passion brings, you won't be so quick to mistake someone else's idea of Profit for your own.

Even when you are confident that the Profit you are

seeking comes from your heart, you can be surprised by the unforeseen benefits that sometimes result. This is what happened for a neighbor of mine who, after letting passion guide him, found new resolve and unexpected freedom. Alan had been working as an executive in an advertising firm in Miami for three years. He had been dating his girlfriend, Pamela, for four years. He lived in an upscale apartment with ocean views, drove a fancy car, and by all appearances had a great life. Under the surface, however, Alan was troubled. He felt his opportunities to progress at work were limited and did not enjoy working under the tutelage of a sometimes egomaniacal boss. Moreover the type of work he was doing had become less and less fulfilling over the past months. Until then, Alan had been afraid to leave his job; he felt that, at thirty-five, he must be conservative and responsible in his career decisions. Despite the supposed safety the job afforded him, he did not feel secure enough in his future to ask his girlfriend to marry him. She had moved out of the apartment a year before because of his reluctance. He was trapped by confusion and dissatisfaction.

Gradually things came into focus for Alan, and with a single decision he changed the course of his life completely. He looked to his passion. He knew that what he really wanted to do, what he really loved to do, was take pictures. He had pursued photography avidly as a hobby, but had been afraid to make the jump to professional status. He also knew that given his industry contacts and what he considered fair talent, he had a decent shot at success. So he decided to spend a few months getting advice and putting together a plan before quitting his job. As the weeks went by he began to feel liberated from his old fears. He made a down payment on the house he had been afraid to buy. And most important, he called his mom in St. Louis and had her help him find a ring—an engagement ring.

Alan probably never imagined the consequences that would stem from the single decision to pursue his passion. Not everyone's life will come together in such well-timed or fortunate fashion, but the example he provides is instructive. He profited in ways he never imagined by opening himself to his passion. He may or may not make it as a photographer, but he has found success in other areas of his life where before there was only frustration.

THE PASSION CYCLE

By now you have probably learned that passion and Profit are closely linked. I hope it is obvious to you that passion is the single most important factor in realizing your Profit. I also hope you understand that the process of following passion to Profit is not linear but a cycle (see Figure 10.1) that repeats itself time and again. When you follow your passion to one level of Profit, you are invigorated; your passion is renewed and perhaps recreated. As your existing passions evolve and new passions emerge based on the Profit you find, you are then inspired to reach even higher levels of Profit.

PASSIONEERING

If you remain steadfast in your commitment to your passion, eventually this cycle will become second nature for you. You will no longer dwell on the individual steps, rather they will

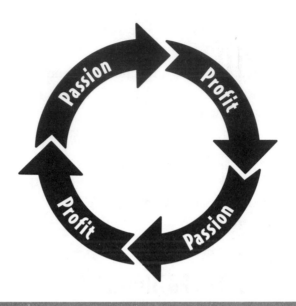

Figure 10.1. Passion Cycle.

become a self-sustaining part of your life, the dynamic that determines the choices you make and the actions you take. In this sense you will transcend any plan I, or anyone else, can offer you. You will become self-actualizing, having a heightened knowledge of who you are and what you can and should accomplish. You alone will understand what is best for you, and the steps you can take to make it happen. You will build the future you have dreamed of by allowing what is best and most inspiring in you to break free. You will become a passioneer.

Always remember that within you are the seeds of your happiness, your accomplishment, and your personal greatness. Remember also that no one else can give these things to you; you must find them yourself. To do so I tell you this: look to your passion for inspiration, follow it to fulfillment.

References

Campbell, J., and Moyers, B. *The Power of Myth*. (B. S. Flowers, ed.). New York: Anchor, 1988.

Carroll, L. *Alice's Adventures in Wonderland* and *Through the Looking Glass*. New York: Bantam, 1981 [1861].

Coehlo, P. *The Alchemist*. (A. Clarke, trans.). New York: HarperFlamingo, 1998.

Csikszentmihalyi, M. *Flow: The Psychology of Optimal Experience*. New York: Harper, 1991.

Csikszentmihalyi, M. *Finding Flow*. New York: Basic Books, 1997.

Dickinson, E. *Final Harvest: Emily Dickinson's Poems*. (Selections and introduction by T. H. Johnson.) Boston: Little, Brown, 1961 [1870].

Disraeli, B. *Coningsby: Or, the New Generation*. New York: Penguin, 1993 [1884].

Gibran, K. *The Prophet*. New York: QPBC, 1995 [1923].

Hegel, G.W.F. *Philosophy of History*. (J. Sibree, trans.) New York: Dover, 1956 [1832].

Holmes, O. W. Jr. Memorial Day Address, 1884.

James, W. *The Writings of William James*. (J. J. McDermott, ed.). University of Chicago Press, 1977 [1902].

Maslow, A. *Toward a Psychology of Being*. (2nd ed.). Princeton, N.J.: Van Nostrand, 1968.

Shakespeare, W. *King Henry V*. In *Complete Works of William Shakespeare*. New York: Avenel, 1975 [1599].

Thoreau, H. D. *Walden*. New York: Penguin, 1986 [1854].

Warshaw, M. "Get a Life." *Fast Company*, June–July 1998, pp. 138–150.

Warshaw, M. "Keep It Simple." *Fast Company*, June–July 1998, pp. 154–160.